THE ANONYMOUS MYSTIC

Written by Judy Fraser
Spiritual Psychotherapist

Also available by the same author:

Second Aid

The Soul Searcher

ISBN-13: 978-9197987530
ISBN-10: 9197987530

CONTENTS

JUDY FRASER

ACKNOWLEDGMENTS

This book is dedicated to:

THE GREAT BEINGS FROM THE INVISIBLE REALMS WHO CHOSE TO INSTRUCT ME, TO WHOM I HUMBLY GIVE THANKS EACH AND EVERY DAY, AND TO MY FAMILY WHO CONTINUE TO TEACH ME SO MUCH

Keith Hall, Proofreader, Editor
Richard White from Word Edit
Pavllou Landraagon Kokko, ClearHorse Design & Image

JUDY FRASER

FOREWORD

There can be no doubt that the planet is changing, our very existence on this great Earth is in transit, and even science acknowledges that the very stardust that falls to earth is instrumental in our DNA changing and evolving.

Therefore the spiritual counterpart to the physical home must also change as we move through these challenging times. It seems that there is a greater spiritual divide, between those that choose dark places and those that wish to move into the light and shine a torch for others to follow.

For me, real Spirituality is how we live in our everyday world; how we bring our spiritual beliefs into the ordinary. That is always our real test. Spirituality exists in a simple act, word or deed, whether dark or light. To be human is to sometimes fail, dust ourselves off and then try again, but always aiming to get it right.

Judy Fraser is a rare being, someone who has been able to traverse spiritual knowledge, live it, and generously create a map for others to follow, shining a torch for others, when it gets just too dark to see, no matter what colour, culture or religion. She gives us sublime practices that, if followed correctly, will align us to our Destiny and not our Fate.

I am delighted to publish Judy Fraser's books. How she formulates the MU's work shows us a practical way forward in order to push us all through a difficult time. Her generosity and humility are refreshing in this age of the Spiritual jumble sale.

My advice is to read her books and then read them again and again and each time you will find something new. Keep them handy.

Pavllou Landraagon Kokko

JUDY FRASER

INTRODUCTION

The book you are about to read has its origins in my personal experiences and journey. With four children, an absent husband meant being a single woman and a single parent to three young children and one teenager. It required meditation just to stay sane!

There often comes a point in our lives where we reach a vacuum, that stage where our history is filled with pain and we want to avoid repeating it, and meditation can help us lay down a new blueprint, one on which we can build a much more positive future. Of course, laying that foundation and trying to build upwards from it takes time, persistence, discipline, trust and acceptance, and there are many peaks and troughs that we must navigate successfully. Unfortunately in today's society, the suggestion for many people, male or female, would be a prescription for a chemical drug to "get you through this difficult time." People forget that those pills do nothing except mask the symptoms, dumb your senses down so you feel immune to the world. But why? It is something I cannot quite relate to; yes, I can fully empathise with the idea that something needs to change so that I can just feel normal again, but what eludes me is the desire to detach oneself from the real world. The real world is amazing! Its natural beauty rivals any drug, in my opinion. We have at our disposal the experiences, writings, theories and discoveries from all of history, just a click away with the Internet. Our friends and family have the ability to grow every day, not just in stature but in intelligence and maturity, humour and graciousness. It's true that not all do grow, instead opting for a more destructive path, but why would anyone want to miss out on that?

So I suppose I consider myself somewhat lucky to possess the mentality that I have; that my disposition was not to look for a quick fix to my problems, but to find the right fix. Although in truth, I did not always feel that way; for some time I believed that my mentality was a curse, and I pondered the possibility that I had made rebellion my profession. Thankfully, hindsight, as it so often does, showed me the blessing later on, and I want to pass my experience on so others can avoid the feeling of uncertainty about their lives. The question is not, "How can I take a short cut out of this difficult time?" but "How can I embrace this life that I have created, so that I may enjoy it fully and cope effectively, without missing out on the many joys and surprises within?"

Once you ask that question, well, my friend, that is when the fun begins! It does not matter if you are a single parent or not; it matters not one iota if you are male or female, young or old, atheist or Christian, educated or uneducated. What matters is that you realise life is a glorious thing with untold treasures to offer, and the best way through it is to embrace it, to see the endless beauty and good within it, and to find out how to get the most out of life.

That is what this book is all about – showing you how to become the best version of yourself, far in excess of what you ever thought was possible, and making the most out of the life that you have been given. The content of this book is concise, so you may dip in and out of it for reference and glean the important stuff without being bogged down with superfluous information.

Have an open mind, an open heart, and see how spectacular the universe is. This book comes from my personal journey, and reading it will reveal yours, so make the most of it and remember the three Es:

embark, enable, embrace!

1
THE BODY AS OUR TEMPLE

The body is a complex machine, and while it lacks the same moving components of a car, as one example, it still works in extraordinary and unusual ways. The primary emotion of fear, for instance, which we all feel at regular and often frequent times in our life, is stored in the glandular system. In order to overcome fear we require courage – to face the fear head-on or to simply find a way to circumnavigate it; whichever path we decide to take, the courage required can lead us to feel lousy: weak, despondent, perhaps ill. Such feelings make it difficult to continue because they act as negative reinforcement, i.e. that we are doing something wrong. This is far from true, though, and the reason courage makes us feel lousy is because the energy it requires has to come from somewhere; as we can't just make it at will, so it is borrowed from our physical side as a temporary measure until we are able to re-stabilise. Taking away energy from the physical side leaves us with the usual symptoms of depleted energy, in the same way that we feel depleted after engaging in physical exercise. While it may be startling at first, it is important not to make the mistake of thinking it's permanent: it is a temporary feeling, but the human mind is so powerful that if we think it will be permanent then it will be, and it is this that can result in a diagnosis of M.E.

In order to move beyond this, we need to follow the typical rules on increasing energy: consume wholesome and nutritious food, exercise to get our hormones in good balance and our body generally used to exertion, and lots of sleep to facilitate rest and recuperation. Once we stabilise, we will feel like our normal selves again and have the added bonus of new wisdom and strength, both of which we can offer as gifts to anyone who wants them.

At any given point in life we can experience stress, worry or doubt. Doubt can be particularly troublesome as we can start to second-guess our actions or decisions in life, especially around such issues as partnerships, work or money. When we decide to take note of, and adhere to, the Management Upstairs (which is the terminology for a higher power used throughout this book), we need to simply get on with it. If we hesitate or lack trust, we will find ourselves stagnating. Therefore, the appropriate course of action is to take notice of the Management Upstairs, trust it and listen to the incoming messages, as we learn to surrender ourselves to it completely.

Initially we fall into a catatonic state in the hope our body will feel relaxed and comforted. Then we begin to think we are losing the plot and are a danger to ourselves and to others. We freak ourselves and others out and feel impotent and frustrated as a result. We have to learn how to discipline the mind as well as the body. Then we action life in ways that are new to us and work to be as relatively harmless towards ourselves and others as is possible.

Those with faith in religion often acknowledge that we, as humans, are still rather ignorant on matters of the universe and life as a wider topic. So it is particularly important to surrender to the Management Upstairs and have faith that it knows more than we do, that it can see the bigger picture before it unfolds. As we are on the ground floor it is too easy to be short-sighted and see only what is immediately before us, and this makes it difficult to trust in our decisions that impact heavily on the future. By relinquishing control to the higher power we can simply get on with what we need to do, without the constant burden of worrying what we should be doing instead. By doing so, we should feel a weight lifted from our shoulders, as the responsibility of figuring out what to do is given up to someone else.

Relinquishing control to the Management Upstairs does not absolve us of all responsibility, though; indeed, part of the education is learning that it is a joint effort, we are not being spoon-fed but employing the generous light that is being offered. At any given point in life something can go wrong, from a crack in the wall to a broken washing machine, and we know to have these issues fixed as and when they occur, without thinking we need help from a higher power. This is evidence of us knowing what to do, and acting in a proactive manner. This is important to maintain – growth will not occur if we try to simply shift all responsibility elsewhere; rather you just need to have confidence that our problems, be they monetary or physical or emotional, will be taken care of. The Management Upstairs will be testing our validity to check our commitment and our current stage, to determine how far along we are in our journey.

Generally, the journey is one constant process; we recharge as we go, with sleep and specified mineral and nutrient intake helping us, which means we get no build-up and so can continue progressing. However, everything needs to go harmoniously in the proper balance and so there may be times when we are forced to slow down or stop entirely, reflect on the past and wait to be given the green light to move forward once again. When work is being done in the head, this, spiritually speaking, will be one of the times that our journey will temporarily stagnate. The head being as complex as it is, the time taken to work on it can vary but may take quite some time, and during this period it is wise to include a daily mineral supplement in our diet and ensure we get proper rest each night, as this will facilitate the process and reduce the time before we are told we can once again put one foot in front of the other.

It can be difficult to find the time to meditate, especially when life is so hectic it feels as though the only time we have time to ourselves is when we are asleep or trying to unwind. It is at these times that it is important to communicate with the Management Upstairs; by doing so, we will be met with light and see the way forward. Armed with this knowledge, we can release the fear presented by the darkness that is the past, knowing that we are moving smoothly and rapidly. Although it can be hard to find time to meditate, it is ideal to do it twice a day; the actual times of day are not of particular importance, but it would be best to *be regular.* In the morning we receive, in the evening we feed back. The benefit of this is that we will find ourselves progressing faster, which will of course be most welcome during difficult phases. The Management Upstairs will inform us of when the difficult times will be over, such as one or two days, and it always delivers on its promises, but we need to understand that time in the universal worlds differs vastly from time on earth so if a day is quoted it is not an earth day as we understand it to be. So if we find ourselves in a tricky place but are instructed that it will be over shortly, do not fall behind as a result of the problem, but forge ahead and before we know it we will be out the other side.

At any given time, we are in a period of change and, just like when businesses enter a period of transition, it takes time to become re-established and grounded to move forward again. Businesses make people redundant and a similar process happens in the personal realm too, so it may be confusing to know who to hold on to and who to let go as you keep evolving. All will become clear in a relatively short space of time though, so try not to be distracted with trivial matters such as this.

During the process of spiritual evolution we can experience a range of emotions, not all of them positive. It is important to respond to these emotions in the manner we desire; if we feel like shouting, we must shout; if we feel like swearing and crying then swear and cry we should. As unpleasant as these feelings may be, they are normal and the Management Upstairs will constantly be showing that we cannot lose contact with it, that it will always be there to guide us regardless of how we behave. So although we constantly strive to improve we must also recognise where we are right now and take responsibility not to hurt or harm another deliberately.

What always needs to be remembered is that this is a process, and not necessarily a quick one. We may at times find ourselves in a state of unrest, and before continuing we will need to move into a better state. The Management Upstairs will of course aid us with this, and even a state of unrest can be managed and the Management Upstairs will help to speed things up wherever possible. While we will be receiving outside help, we can also help ourselves and one way of doing so is by consuming the right things. For instance, pure foods and drinks like salads, bread and water for a few days will help, and avoiding tea and biscuits in this time will be of benefit. After this period of cleansing we can go back to consuming more of what we feel we need.

We will soon begin noticing changes, not just physical and mental changes but in our life as a whole, too. For instance, people will stop bothering us like they did before, instead they will approach us for help, advice, comfort and guidance; and no longer will we be in need of constant encouragement, instead we will be the one offering that to others. In order to get to that point, though, we need to be careful with what we say about people. If we disapprove of someone's actions we must remain quiet and act as though we do not have an opinion. It is misguided to believe that others will keep opinions a secret and we do not want or need comments coming back to haunt us, so instead we need only to look at others and love them. We are free to say whatever we want, with the only caveat being it is with praise, gratitude and humour, nothing sinister, harmful or otherwise negative.

Also during these periods of change we may be instructed to remain somewhat isolated, and this is because the Management Upstairs may want to keep our energy separate from those of others until the process is complete, as well as the fact that certain people's energies can frustrate or annoy us and raise disharmony which we are trying to free ourselves from. It will not take long, so during these times we will need to stay home and keep ourselves entertained as best we can.

This period of isolation can cause confusion as to who our friends really are. As briefly mentioned above, changes occur in our personal lives regarding who to hold on to and who to let go of, and we may find ourselves at a different junction whereby old friends are gone, but new ones have not yet arrived, putting us in a position of mixing transitory acquaintances. As ever, the thing to do at this point is simply be patient and wait in the void; don't spend too much time reminiscing on old friends or trying to prolong a friendship that shouldn't be, and don't get too caught up in the friends we have at present that will not be around for long. Both of these actions waste both energy and our own resources, and the best thing to do is just wait for the permanency to settle in. However, do not make the mistake of thinking that all old friendships need to be severed for us to progress – many people have lifelong friendships and there is no reason that we shouldn't too, but at the same time do not try to force friendships just for nostalgia. Using the same analogy as before of a business making people redundant, no business will let all of its employees go and employ a whole new workforce, because only some will need to be trimmed for the benefit of the company. The same is true in our personal life: some friends may need to be left in the past, but others can be just as beneficial going forward as they have been previously, so while it's important not to try to hold onto a friendship for nostalgia, it is equally important to maintain friendships that ought to be maintained and not let people go under the false assumption that starting afresh or progressing personally means cutting all ties with the past.

Once we are through with the isolation period and have completed the level we are currently on, we will need another period of rest to restore our energy and settle down in our new spiritual place, which will then facilitate our moving onto the next level. The reason for the rest and time to settle down is that the journey is quite difficult and involves much strain, for us and those around us, so it is crucial that everyone is given time to get back into a routine before disrupting the status quo again. We will at this stage be given our freedom and, thanks to our progression, our peers will begin to regard us as a leader. If we have been facing troubles with work or money, we should find that at this point the barriers are removed and the troubles disappear along with them.

Having moved from one level to another, the process will in some ways feel like being back at square one, although we will know more of what to expect as time goes on. However, when we are being worked with to progress we may find ourselves feeling faint, so ensure you are eating every two hours and never skip a meal. It should be evident by now that resting and maintaining our strength are hugely important factors in our spiritual quest, and eating is of course a huge component of that. Therefore, it is imperative that we maintain regular eating habits and do not go without food. There are times this can be difficult, so if you think you will find yourself in such a situation that eating will be problematic, take some food with you or set a timer to remind yourself to find something to eat; the last thing you need is to feel weak or unwell as a result of not having adequate energy. As with all these things, though, this will only last for a short period of time. If you lead a particularly busy lifestyle with no time to yourself, you may find that the Management Upstairs helps to arrange a few minutes for us to spend alone each evening so that our journey can continue unabated, but our responsibility is to not take on more than we can handle and only bite off what we can chew. During the journey we need to remind ourselves that we are also allowed to have fun and enjoy ourselves, because we may not have had much opportunity to do the things that we enjoy; we may not even know what they are currently.

If we are in a difficult position in terms of employment then we may find that we will not get another job, but will instead be put to work for the Management Upstairs in various ways, such as being prompted to talk of our beliefs and ideas to people in industry clubs, as well as students in sixth forms and colleges. We become known to them through an event that we will by this stage be ready for, before which we will be primed to be able to communicate with the Management Upstairs in a similarly natural way as we talk to people in everyday life. By this point all of our higher senses will be working properly, and all we will be waiting for is an official seal of approval that allows us to properly make use of our skills to support and help others.

When you go to bed each night let go of the day as best you are able and just relax. If you really can't sleep do not worry about it; if need be get up have a cup of tea and do something you enjoy or need to do before returning to bed. If you just lie there thinking about not sleeping you will get frustrated. The natural balance will be restored in the fullness of time. It is important to remember that as we move on to the next level we will not be used to the changing pace and so will not be entirely comfortable. As always, avoid worrying and place faith in the higher power that our body's vibrations will soon be back in tune. In the meantime, we can facilitate things by practicing our breathing exercises each day; a useful exercise is to breathe in for four seconds, hold for two, exhale for four, hold for two, and repeat this for as many times as you are comfortable with. While it may seem like a trivial exercise, it is important to help us during the times when we are undergoing rearrangement and do not feel as good as usual. It is a useless exercise if not done naturally, so don't focus all concentration onto counting how long we are inhaling and exhaling; ensure we also focus on breathing naturally with our body's mechanism.

There is also a possibility than the Management Upstairs will want us in another venue to make use of the facilities there, so do not panic if you get unwell or have to go to hospital for tests for a day or so. It will not always be sinister or involve a need for surgery – our visit may simply be one of observation so the Management Upstairs can use the equipment in the hospital to magnify or boost energy. The Management Upstairs will also care for any responsibilities in our personal life, such as children, so we must not concern ourselves with our personal affairs while away from usual routines.

There will be times on our journey that parts of our body may ache or be painful, the reason being that different parts of our body are affected by different things spiritually and emotionally, so as emotional channels are cleansed we might feel something physically or not understand what is going on. To overcome the physical symptoms, there are some things we can do besides waiting for them to disappear naturally. Firstly, listen to instruction from the Management Upstairs, as it will have clear guidelines for us to follow to facilitate the process. Secondly, relax; read books, take care of our home and try not to worry about life in general. These things are our contribution to progression; we might find ourselves making friends with new people, and they can help by lending or giving us books that are conducive to our progress.

*

It is important to learn at least the basics about levels beyond our current understanding. God, or whatever you like to call the higher powers, is made up of various dimensions of light. We serve that sphere we are on while reaching to next level as we journey to reach the next level. The Management Upstairs is also there to help us with things that we are unable to do, such as activating centres, and this requires us to cooperate. It is for this reason that instructions are so important: we acquire knowledge from a person assigned or from books and we can therefore know what to expect, thus lessening the shock that we would otherwise feel. This allows the progress to happen faster and it is easier for us to adapt to. The facilitator we are assigned we may not recognise or even like; they come in varying sizes and may or may not be dressed in holy robes.

Imagine that the Management Upstairs is a gardener and you are a seed that has been planted to raise the vibration of the Earth. We are part of a team but the other team members are busy, so we must work alone while we find out whether we are to stay in this team or move to another one. We are now equipped with the wisdom and knowledge for our revised work to begin, and our work is to bring to people's attention that they need to study themselves before they begin on others. The way forward will always be shown to us, and our health must be of a certain level. As we ready ourselves to move we either lose or gain weight; to provide buoyancy we may gain, or if we have let go of issues we have been hanging onto we lose weight for no apparent reason. This will mean the Management Upstairs will not need to create a scenario that focuses our attention, so the action of re-direction can be understood. If it isn't the instruction will get progressively more concentrated until we do understand what is required. We will always be taken care of but we do not always understand how immediately! We will be able to speculate, even understand through activation of clairaudience and clairvoyance, but we must take notice of prompts. These abilities will be bestowed on us all at once so we will require time to adjust; although we will be protected we will also need to be wary so we do not suffer any excess shock. At times we will be cleansed, which will slow us down and give the Management Upstairs a chance to put its revising plans into operation. Always remember that even if we feel sluggish or unwell, it is all part of our moving forward and progressing, and no matter how bad things feel, we will never be abandoned.

We may also experience problems with our joints, but again it is nothing to be alarmed about. The Management Upstairs will release minute electrons into our body that will permit us to see and communicate directly with what is going on at a physical level, and this can manifest itself as a joint disorder to begin with. It will be an unpleasant and painful experience, but it is both necessary and temporary, so we just try to ride it through the best we can. We can, if we think it will help, see a doctor, who may administer blood tests, but remember that it a part of the process and we are fine. Perhaps you will prefer a chiropractor, an acupuncturist or a reflexology session. Now rather than obstructing the process we start to harmonise with it and cooperate with changing and being changed rather than obstructing it. Now we make it easier for the Management Upstairs to work on us in the necessary ways. The Management Upstairs has to make adjustments to us at certain periods so that they remain in constant communication with us, so surrender to whatever is presented to us in our day-to-day life and emerge stronger as a result. Always remember that the discomfort is temporary, but the benefits are permanent. Once complete, we will live multi-dimensionally and eventually after our apprenticeship we become one of the workers in service to those we meet. We will of course still live on Earth, but we will have entered the next level of being so be able to cover more ground. By this time we will have achieved a number of things:

- We will have relived our memories and cleared everything that we need to.
- The planning will be complete and our body will be ready, so the Management Upstairs can reach us any time it is necessary.
- We will be able to link well and quickly.
- We have a realistic viewpoint rather than an idealistic, and we have retained the essence of all we need having enabled effluence to be recycled at every level of being.

There will then be a period of about a couple of years where we will simply rest. This time is required to recover, repair old damage and recuperate from the increased negative charge. As negative charge is being introduced we need the time to work through it. Our eating habits may change, we may eat less or be ravenous so we just need to be sensible and live simply. We will be guided throughout, so never feel alone; if in doubt link into the body and ask what it requires. As work is undertaken we will feel pains and aches in different parts of our body, including our hips, shoulders, elbows, wrists, knees, ankles, fingers, toes, neck and head, so expect some discomfort as this takes place, and get help or rest as it is required.

The purpose of the work being done with us is to enable us to receive 'the gift of god'. It is so called because we will begin to see into other people and perhaps feel their feelings, or hear what they are saying when not in our presence, and as these are such powerful gifts they must never be used incorrectly or abused. In order to receive our gift, in addition to the changes already detailed, we must pass a test of faith, and the light of knowledge gained. Once we have passed the tests we will always be able to contact the Management Upstairs directly, and from there we will learn how to pass information on without giving offence to the people we are supposed to message. Having understood all that is necessary, we can go onward as we learn humility, modesty, love and compassion in service; and we will be free to follow our own path and there will be no more barriers in this turn of the spiral.

One of the most repeated lessons in this book is to rest and recover, and that also extends to not working too much as we leave an old episode and connect to the new. This does not mean we avoid hard work – we must work hard to achieve and be fulfilled in what we do, but we should not over-exert ourselves. If we do, we will simply slow ourselves down because we will then need to stop and recover whereas we otherwise would have progressed at a regular and continuous pace. Perhaps it will be within a relationship, a work situation, family changes or relocations. Whatever it is we need to realign.

We need to meditate and to listen prior to seeing the new way. We will get a response although not always at the time of asking. Then we contemplate the way to go and if we ask we will find we begin to receive help in the most unlikely ways. We need to maintain our awareness. Along the same lines, if we find ourselves having trouble walking, such as knee or hip trouble, or keeping our balance that is an indication of further changes being introduced at a physical level. We need to remind ourselves to have patience!

Checklist:

- Is your body in need of some help? Are you unwell? Aching? Fatigued? Ask yourself do you need help from a doctor, dentist, alternative practitioner or optician. Whatever you decide do it!
Does your diet agree with you? Do you need to drink more water? Do you need to cleanse?
- Do you need to exercise? Where, at the gym, in the fields, mountains, by lakes or the ocean? Ask inside yourself and then action today.
- Do you need to take time out? Read a novel, see a movie, listen to music.
- Don't think about it do it!
- Do you need to find a class in yoga, Pilates or martial arts or get a personal trainer to plan a program for you which you can keep to day by day? Do something to facilitate physical fitness within your sphere.

2
EMOTIONS, MOTIVATE AND MAGNIFY

When the journey first begins and the Management Upstairs begin to focus on supervising our development they will enter our aura; it will be an unfamiliar sensation for us and may lead to symptoms such as headaches, toothaches or nausea. As with all the 'negative' feelings throughout the process, this is just temporary and is nothing to be concerned about. We may also sometimes hear sounds, perhaps similar to that of a mouse squeaking or a sudden cracking that we can't account for. These are just the noises of the unfamiliar and they are an illusion, one that draws our attention; we can always ask them to stop at any time if it becomes too much to bear too soon.

Sometimes we feel that no one cares for us or loves us, but the Management Upstairs do and always have. Some of us take a long time to overcome the feelings of rejection and abandonment experienced at birth when we separated from the invisible realm. We may have agreed and even been counselled what to expect but we conveniently forget and so complain loud and long. If we are able to overcome the hatred and smother it in love, that extends for miles, not only to those we love and care for on the Earth, but it also calls back those who counsel and care for us and who just wait for our call. This will help us feel connected, more complete, and well cared for. Only when we ask do we receive! Until that time we are left to fend for ourselves. This is why some have to become fairly desperate before overcoming their pride and realising that help is needed. We may have been disappointed and disillusioned, having asked for help from those we know, before being prompted to ask for help beyond the familiar.

One key lesson is that self-indulgence is not tolerated. We all need to recognise self-indulgence in ourselves and in others, and there can be no denying that it is difficult to find a balance, but find it we must. If there is a situation that requires us to use ourselves as the complainant then it is perfectly valid, but we have to drop the self-indulgence and surround ourselves in light. This is the way in which people become convinced of our strength, especially when it has risen out of vulnerability and personal experience.

At this stage of the journey we will be learning to control our energy levels, and already we will be better than we were before. Often it is only when we look back that we realise how much we have changed and been changed; that is why we need time to catch up with ourselves. This means we will trust the Management Upstairs more – which is essential to a successful and pleasant progression, along with acceptance and the ability to let go of the past and a projected future and just be here in the present moment. There is an energy mass that surrounds us, and our lack of an inflated ego permits us to communicate in a powerful manner, to a degree that other people who do have strong egos cannot, even if they are more talented or knowledgeable than us and force us to see things their way. We are no longer a victim of circumstance or so afraid; now we are able to stand in our own light knowing we are guarded and guided on the Earth plane by powerful beings working for the good of all. This should also highlight the fact that we all need to utilise our strengths; we should not shy away from something because someone is stronger or knows more about a topic than we do, because our own strengths can give us an advantage that allows us to go farther than our peers. This brings new problems as old groups deform to enable reformation to take place. Not better or worse, just different.

The importance of rest and sleep has already been mentioned, and it is being mentioned again to keep it in the forefront of our minds. A rested body facilitates good growth, whereas tiredness and stress can disrupt the process. At this stage it is particularly important, as the glands will be being worked on by the Management Upstairs and so will not be functioning quite properly. The result of this is that we will be low on energy as we will be carrying a greater load than normal and we will need to readjust to get used to it. We must understand it is the time to let go of the fear, extract what we need from what is no longer required by us and then let romantic ideals go in favour of real opportunities that present themselves. It may seem instant and we may get clues as we begin to understand. The emotions must dramatise the situations so we understand in more detail what is required and then our physical body must catch up and recover. There will also be a greater load to the head centres if our lifestyle is not as peaceful as it could be, so don't be alarmed if that is the case. This will change soon enough too, so we just keep on keeping on. Above all, we maintain our strength by consuming the right foods and getting plenty of rest – we need to build up strong reserves whenever possible because we have so many internal changes taking place on higher levels, which can sap our energy. Strong reserves will help to safeguard against that happening. Be aware also that we need to be stricter about our overall health – keep up a good exercise programme and try to eliminate unhealthy foods from your diet and above all drink lots of water.

*

The journey we have embarked on is also one of education, and we will learn much about the realms of life that most are unaware of. As a result there is much to learn. When and how do we report what we know to others, how do we handle their reactions, when do we keep quiet? At this stage we have more questions than answers.

There is a grid comprising circular magnets, which plugs us into an earth vortex which magnifies all aspects; this history includes the good the not so good and the downright ugly. The grid is not made from one person – but from all aspects, above and below. This magnet acts alone until we are refined and made relatively harmless. If and when this is achieved we have access to another type of ley line, similar to the way threads run in a spider web connecting one edge to another, and we are escorted to another destination. The Management Upstairs supplies the electric force that mobilises us, and we, the person, supply the magnetic force to gather the necessary people together, while the electric magnetism gives the necessary current for activation. This allows people to be linked together, and we can share our wisdom and humour with others, which in turn will also help all move on and progress. We are attracted to new places, people and things as others are rejected. This appears to happen irrespective of our actions when the time comes for all to grow and move on. Our own magnetic energy is at work now, so work hard to emit positive thoughts of love, cooperation and light and joy, as this will help us to attract the same qualities back to us.

By this moment, we can get a sore mouth or throat or a cold. This will be because we are ignorant of our verbal role; it prompts us to keep speaking rather than stopping to listen. We are seeking our new form of expression as we find our updated status. The simple remedy is to refrain from talking when we would usually jump in with our own thoughts, and instead take the time to listen to what is being said by others around us. We may then decide that we do not need to add anything, but if we do want to keep talking we will do so with a stronger foundation than if we had blocked the contribution of others straight away. Eventually others will want to listen; they will monitor the egotistical on our behalf as it is us they want to listen to. Until that time we wait nicely to be shown the way!

It is also important to remember that nobody is perfect – everyone has their flaws, some to a greater degree than others, and we have a substantial load to carry, which can facilitate our imperfections coming to the surface faster than they otherwise might. There is not much that can be done about this other than to keep on keeping on; however we should make a date to have ourselves monitored. A chiropractor or acupuncturist can help balance both back and neck, as this will allow our awareness to be lifted again. Martial arts and yoga can also support us; we just need to make sure we harmonise with those we work with. We can also talk to a friend or a counsellor and mirror our own feelings back to ourselves by talking honestly. We have to make sure they are a safe and open space and not those people who use the opportunity to tell us how we should be and what we should think. The law of multiplicity will then take effect; if we put our faith in our own resources we will soon see the results; our own efforts will be added to those from the more subtle realms. Yet, be careful not to try too hard; it's a pitfall that many fall into when embarking on something new: whether it's a diet or new exercise regime, it invariably leads to the desire to give up. Our health is fine, and variations in our temperature are not signs of illness but are simply the changing rates of vibration; the feeling will not last for ever, it is just something we need to get used to. Not trying too hard also includes relaxation – to enable the Management Upstairs to work to be in contact with us we learn to reach up as they reach down. We need to have firm foundations that can withstand almost any impact, so do not worry about being out of reach while our core is being strengthened.

What we find throughout our spiritual journey is the experience of various emotions. At this early stage, we are apt to feel depressed. This is not our fault, nor is it going to last. It is merely the result of the Management Upstairs 'rearranging' our mind, and it will pass when our new form of expression is found. We will also notice our stomach occasionally requesting a rest, so avoid junk food – eat at the usual times, but try to stick to the healthier, wholesome options.

From this point on we are at work for the Management Upstairs, whenever and wherever we are required. Our link will continue to strengthen on a daily basis and we will no longer have a fear of losing the ability to meditate. Do not think this represents the conclusion of the journey, though! On the contrary; this is to watch how we respond, to see if we will carry on or not as more responsibility is asked of us. If we continue and complete our apprenticeship, we will be accepted and integrated into the hierarchy. Once there, we will be taught secrets of the trade, guaranteeing an interesting and enjoyable future where we will always know that we are loved and needed in many areas. No need to force our presence on those who do not respect or honour us anymore. We only work with those who are willing to learn from us as we are willing to respect and learn from them.

- Who in your circle do you feel very uncomfortable around?
- Do we stay in places that hold a presence or an atmosphere of hostility?
- Where do you feel the need to defend yourself or have a desire to attack?
- Can you look at your face in a mirror and truly like the person you see within it?
- Do you feel the need to dissect yourself or do you see a dignified and holistic status?

3
DETACH, OBSERVE, DISCRIMINATE AND DISCERN

If we take the time to look at nature we will see many lessons. A tree of substance is strong and neither domesticated nor suppressed – it just develops naturally. A tree will sway in the wind, adapting to the conditions because if it remained rigid its branches would snap. We are doing the same thing, so we learn to be at peace with ourselves and let the Management Upstairs support us in improving our quality of life. When we learn to cooperate with the changes taking place within mind and body and learn to cooperate rather than worry or resist, we will see how quickly the work can be completed when necessary.

One area that needs improving is our brain. It has long been known that the left and right sides operate differently and control opposite sides of the body, but these two sides must unite and learn to work together in a common purpose. If the left side and right side are both operational but not working together, our energy will deplete quickly and we will be rather irritable. Usually the right side works with the intuitive, more feminine holistic view, and the left side is the more logical masculine active administrator. If the two sides fight and bicker for who is the more essential we lose the point and self-limit, and this prevents us risking exploring new adventures. If we do manage to acknowledge and unite the two in a common purpose, more material to work with is released through the back of the head, sometimes referred to as the dragon or old brain.

If we get this far then the new day represents a time of cleansing old hurts, old ways of doing things and old expectations. Old methods are often clumsy and ineffective; the more ancient they are the more upgrading and updating must be undertaken. It's worth remembering that we are where we are today because of our past learning, rituals and methods – so if we do not change them, we cannot expect to achieve different results. Methods and expectations become outdated and we need to create or utilise new, more efficient ways, which in turn will make us more effective than we have ever been before. This is often difficult though, and no blame is attached to mistakes as we find the new level required. It will not take long for our awareness to increase; in fact it will happen on a daily basis, as will our sensitivity. A gradual build-up represents healthy growth and excellent progress.

As a component of this part of the journey, we will be receiving a huge inflow of energy and this may cause back pain. This should only last for a day or so and is nothing to be concerned about. We may try to power through while we are experiencing it; if we can't then we need to get help. We are constantly learning throughout the entire process, even when it feels unpleasant. We have all met people who appear to be stuck in the past; they wear old fashioned clothes, seem confused, and they relay old news and refer to things long gone. They are people who were potentially becoming more evolved, or promoted if you prefer, but they did not do the cleansing and got stuck where they were. What a waste - with a little guidance, information and assistance they could have become leaders supporting a community in some way.

Care is necessary for everyone to progress and we are not yet as caring as we could, or would wish, to be. While we are on this Earth there is room for improvement. We may be very skilled in one way and inept in others. This is true even though we are not a deliberately naughty or malicious person, and it simply takes time and concerted effort to change and improve our level of compassion across the board. Our training is to help service fellow humans, but we must also be able to empathise with creatures, and this is why we need to develop into a very caring person; if not, a desire for power or fame and greed can too easily overtake us. We cannot have one rule for us and ours and another for others. Certainly we learn to celebrate differences, be they in cultures, customs or life trends. If we find that this – or any other – task is too difficult, we must link to the

Management Upstairs and we will be supplied with what we need; it may just be we are trying to move too fast. If we are, then our shins may hurt us for no apparent reason. Although perseverance is a key and essential quality, we all need help from time to time.

There are plenty of times in everyone's lives where they feel at a complete loss, and we will all know what this feels like. It may feel depressing and disheartening, but we must wait patiently, utilise the time by resting and regenerating and reminding ourselves that life is good. Another new day is about to dawn in our life and then we will be lifted to new horizons with new areas of work. Take courage and know that each time we experience this we are working towards a new and exciting phase of life.

As our experience grows we will not need to communicate with the Management Upstairs as often as in the earlier stages of the journey, and so our 'talk time' will often change to just once a day. Do not fear though; a bat is an animal of extreme reverence because of its sonar abilities and skills of flying at night, and we are now like a bat – flying at night with the freedom to roam anywhere in the galaxy. There is a universe of magic and wonderment at our fingertips, and within three months we will be wondering how we lived as we did for all those years. We have kept our faith and will be rewarded for it; our energy levels will now be great and our purification will be complete this time around. When we repeat the pattern we will have a better idea where we are within the process. And we have probably attracted friends who have experienced this stage of growth even if from a different standpoint; it is always encouraging to compare notes and to laugh and lighten up as we begin to relax. We will also by now have learned new skills; perhaps we will see things beyond what is considered 'normal', such as the energy fields surrounding people or things. We may hear instructions which may mean we are clairaudient, but we must discern what to listen to and what to ignore as being sub-standard. A good rule of thumb is to work out if what we are being told would potentially benefit all; if it would only improve our life it should be rejected. We may feel things intensely if we touch or are touched, in which case whose information is it, ours or theirs? It might even be being received from a passer-by, so we need time to be able to discern what is what. We will not be an expert and we have a long way to go before blossoming into being particularly effective at the skill being offered. It is up to us to learn to translate these gifts so they benefit those seeking our skills. For those who are not yet ready but are interested, we respond to their questions to the best of our ability without being attached to a result. If they listen and take notice, that is fine, if not, that is equally fine. We operate through invitation and osmosis, which are hugely effective. The Management Upstairs will join in to provide us with the information necessary to pass on to the person enquiring, and will adjust our awareness to assist us whenever we have need. Not least, we need to obey, so as we learn to trust and accept we see proof of how helpful our care has been. By now, our level of understanding has an increased capacity and we are approaching our next stage.

As we continue our journey of growth, we will become so attached to the Management Upstairs that our hands will become their hands, our eyes their eyes, and our work will make use of all abilities; this is sometimes referred to as being over-shadowed. Work on our body will now have been completed on this turn of the evolutionary spiral, which may result in weight loss as well as increased mobility. It will, however, also mean we feel tired, as we have taken an enormous charge. Shortly after, though, we will feel a very different energy and then have the realisation that we are working with the Management Upstairs rather than for them. There will come a time when we feel we don't want to continue, but stick with it – it will never last much longer and the rewards will be more than worth it. If we stay on track, do our best, and honestly say how we feel, after we rebel and overcome the strangeness of conversing with disembodied lightworkers, we settle down. On the nursery slopes, so to speak, there is plenty of encouragement and assurances. As we get more comfortable the instructions are less personal and much clearer. As with school, we are expected to regard and respect our instructors; if we do not, we return to the nursery slope and stay there. This is known as self-limitation. If we are respectful and have a willingness to learn we begin to understand just how fortunate we are. After extensive testing and learning we will be put into an area where we can serve and utilise all of our skills and abilities. There we stay until we are moved on again. We learn to detach ourselves enough to be able to observe dispassionately as we discriminate and work out what is for us and what is for another. No-one can be all things to all people, nor should we be.

It has already been mentioned that we will experience different feelings as we progress, and one such experience may be a lack of bounce, or energy. As always, this is just temporary; its reason is to allow a new type of energy to be introduced into our body. It's an old and wise energy that will help you work to develop new ways of working within our own energy fields and associate with those of others.

We may also find ourselves retaining water and feeling tearful. This will be due to the glands and the nervous systems of the body changing their association with each other. We need to just wait and minimise head pain through the use of sunglasses, or by not watching moving images or rushing around. Another 'side effect' that we may experience is a congested stomach, which will be the result of taking in too much and not letting enough go, so be sure to look at the lighter side of life and try to shed the scenes that weigh you down. This is literally indigestion of living. We no longer want what we once wanted, and our capacities and likes and dislikes are challenging us to change.

Things change relatively rapidly, and we will eventually find ourselves in a near-constant state of meditation. The result of this is that we will no longer need to set so much time aside for a dedicated session of meditation as we have in the past. We will need to make a conscious link every day. And of course we will need to meditate in a dedicated manner when we wish to improve our standard of living the next time, but for now we make our link then live our day. If we find ourselves feeling unwell we have the time and the space to examine and adjust, to discover whether we need more or less prayer, meditation and contemplation. When we pray we are asking for clarity and assistance, when we meditate we are listening for instructions, solutions and encouragement, and when we contemplate we are uniting the forces to the best of our ability for use in the here and now. This work is a great responsibility and there is no turning back from it. The path is irreversible and we have agreed to walk it, but be assured that the Management Upstairs is walking it with you. By joining the pathway we will learn to work much more effectively. This is the purpose behind sacred walks or pilgrimages. As we tour we learn to keep our balance, in spite of unfamiliar extremes.

Also know that by reaching where we have, we are potentially being accepted by the Management Upstairs as a permanent member of staff, which will mean an increased amount of information that we are permitted to witness. Our heart is beating to a new rhythm, having been cleansed and cleared (this is the symbolism behind the bleeding hearts found in many Catholic Churches). Our third eye begins to open much more fully and soon we will have the ability to see both our family and ourselves more clearly – do not assume that we will like all that we see, but take comfort in the knowledge that we will be able to support and help others more effectively now we have had these experiences. Our brain is now in better balance and our life as we have known it is at a point of completion; our feeling of bewilderment is completely natural and to be expected, but we are only confused as we are completing one aspect to start another. We die to the old as we are born to the new. We often get a cold at this time to 'buy' the time for cleansing to occur. Enjoy the respite, it won't last long! Most of us are more accomplished at starting a project, relationship or job, than finishing it by tying up loose ends, saying our goodbyes and researching new areas. We need to work on our weaknesses, so that both finishing and starting are simultaneous.

Steady progression and each 'unlock' will give us greater access to a wider range of colour, sound and experience. One way of working with deepening capacities is to allow them to penetrate one by one. Try to identify with the colour or sound each might have and then play with it inside or try to project it onto a loved object and record any reactions as we let it find a way into the life of the person. Using blue as an example, let it penetrate each pore and then act the part of the tone of the blue you choose; the shade can become lighter or darker than before. This can help you understand just what is happening day by day.

Each time a new phase is initiated, we have to learn and practise the nuts and bolts until they become second nature to us. This grants us the ability to speak with understanding as well as knowledge on the subject. This means our infancy is over; now we can find the new expression at throat level and we now represent the higher centres as well as the lower ones. We can link to the Management Upstairs on more than a remote basis – we can cross-check with an audio or visual link. This makes our next stop more realistic when we realise that we now need a strong base to take off from or return to, as well as consideration and loyalty amongst colleagues.

Imagine a group of three thistles. One is dead, one no longer in flower, and the last one is in bud, just waiting to surpass all the clump. The third one represents our current position. Another way of imagining it is by observing the human body – an ear hears sound but cannot speak, and a mouth speaks but cannot hear, therefore both are required for action despite their operating independently of each other. They complement each other. The story here is that even when you feel dejected and in need, others will still need you.

*

We will need to understand a little more about anchoring ourselves to the Earth. We may already have tried to find out about this but have been unable because people have been trying to observe it independently, rather than in relation to people and their surroundings.

One way to picture it is as lots of spiders' webs which are horizontally placed, all joined vertically on each level. If you were to pick up on one level and move it to another level, everything in its path would be affected. There are energies in certain places on Earth that are directly earthed from the Management Upstairs' location, and any person can be discovered by it because we each emit a sound. The Management Upstairs is able to locate the nearest vortex and from there locate the person in question. Certain tribal cultures organise a 'sing back' if someone goes missing and the tribe do not know where they are; they start a sing back and before long the missing person walks back into the tribal homeland.

A higher team looks after each one of us, and that team can link us into a vortex temporarily when necessary, which means we can still be reached even if we are away from our regular place.

Our ability to concentrate and focus can be used to pass beyond our own previous limit, which enables us to reach into the universal brain, or shared unconsciousness, at will. When we are in doubt about something, we pass it to the brain of the Greater; if it is for the benefit of all concerned then we will be granted automatic and immediate access, while if it is for our own interest alone, we will be checked first, similar to passport control when we try to enter another country without the correct papers.

In order to encourage total loyalty from us towards the Greater, there is another, more difficult, task at hand: that is to link to selected minds only. This is now a real possibility for us and the 'pool' into which we may dip comprises many minds, so we must exercise our powers of discernment and discrimination to find a suitable team with whom we work. We can select as many as we feel we need – the final decision is entirely ours; all those we select will simply be joined together by the Greater in order to benefit everyone. If it does not do this, certain people become unavailable; if our choices are good and have been understood correctly we're freed to move on. We will be blessed with auditory and visual perception, and these gifts will permit us to understand people's problems much better than we could previously. Our level of communication will also improve as we request entry, so the Greater Beings believe us and will open the door to assist us through. We take as many people as we are able through with us.

The Management Upstairs is concerned with the level of communication in the world, and the mechanics of speech, and allied senses, must be re-examined. In addition to the ears and mouth, providing the senses of hearing and taste respectively, there is the complete body, which has many more sensory abilities. As we are able to begin to take responsibility for acting as receivers as well as the transmissions we put into the central pool so we can become quite disorientated. We can no longer talk from our desired level, instead we have to consider the merit of our transmission, then make the decision on whether the material should or should not have our information censored; in addition, we must deal with any interference or static pressures, so we will quickly learn to process all information rapidly and effectively.

It will also be necessary to examine other possibilities, i.e. noise levels, tones, as well as gestures, body language, physical expressions and the like. We will be able to recognise new areas of touch and feelings, and we notice that a person who dislikes being touched is often a person in a vulnerable state, one who is fearful of disintegration, whereas the person who wants to be touched constantly is in need of comfort. We smell atmospheres to assess how safe they are for us to be within. We proceed with caution as it can be deemed rude if we walk away for no apparent good reason. As there is a chance of conflict, we try to tread carefully. We will soon learn to think on our feet and handle potentially volatile situations with more aplomb, but in the meantime we learn to be aware of our audience.

There is also actual speech, and this is where we decide whether or not we agree with what is being said. If we disagree then our reserves are made ready and we dismiss another's viewpoint as politely as we can. On the other hand, if we agree then our senses are now harmoniously working together but be aware that our prime sense will not be audio-visual. If the orator is well informed and presents in a low-key and light manner then all levels will work together and harmonisation begins. Conversely, if the orator is unsure and hesitant then the recipient will be on guard, and this will delay harmonisation because the information must be checked through each and every sense before a decision can be made.

The prevailing environmental conditions must also be examined; it is, of course, easy to process information when relaxed in a warm, comfortable, pleasant room, but it is not quite so easy when we are cold, wet and hungry. Each individual must take responsibility for the decision they make to decide whether to proceed or not even when the conditions make it difficult to receive. The decision must be based partly on the concentration and commitment levels of both the orator and the recipient, because both need to be providing something. Consider this fact: the best orator in the world cannot persuade an uninterested receiver to either hear or understand, and so both self-motivation and self-discipline are necessary. The only time we take responsibility for another is when the other is too young, old or vulnerable physically or emotionally to decide for themself. It is a fine line and a difficult one to tread.

With our newfound information and ability, we will be a candle that all at once becomes a furnace – no longer a small light that illuminates the immediate vicinity, but now a large and powerful floodlight lighting the path for many.

We will sense that at this difficult time of testing our endurance levels a new discipline is being established as an older one is coming to an end. Now new, different ways of working will be introduced to you. The planet is our oyster, now we ask ourselves are we a pearl who is willing to become a part of a unit as a small facet within an infinite cosmos; or are we going to try to benefit ourselves only? We are being offered a new beginning, one that is being presented to us, but it requires us to learn to live in a different style. Our endurance levels were tested to the maximum, so don't be surprised that we are exhausted. We need time to rest and recover.

Our soul spirit link is now as fully and unconditionally operational as it can be at this time. This means that we will never be shut off from contact. All magnetic activity is started by an electric thrust, and that thrust is now effective so the magnetic attraction will follow. Prayer is necessary to allow the dimensions to be bridged, so that the one above can assist the one below, and if contact is not made all stay in their respective dimensions.

Our new life is so different, the way ahead is clear, uncluttered, illuminated, beautiful and in motion. Goodness is now an agreeable duty, and the Management Upstairs will now bestow new circumstances into your atmosphere, we are changing and being changed, like it or not!

- Do you trust yourself to be able to work out what is for you and what belongs to someone else?
- Can you stand back from what appears a chaotic situation to be able to see it more clearly?
- Are you able to make your own decision and leave others to make theirs without interference?
- Are you waiting to be shown, or trying to make others see things your way as you try to control or manipulate circumstances?
- Are you allowing yourself to be shown unattached to a projected result?

4
LET GO AND ALL WILL BE MADE NEW

By now work will be starting from the higher level – the level from which the Management Upstairs are operating. For work to begin, the Management Upstairs must open our brain (not literally, of course!) so that it is ready to receive the necessary information. Our ears, eyes and nose are all ready and primed to receive, but our mouth and nerve endings will be in need of a little more 'fine tuning'. On the whole, though, we are in a good enough state and progress will be moving rapidly. But the consequence of all this work is that we are likely to feel under the weather for a while. To be clear, we will not be ill; we just may not feel as spritely as we do usually. The work in the pineal gland may affect our throat, for instance, and the way to treat this is to soothe it to the best of our ability and wait for the discomfort to pass.

We have been briefed on Earth energies and ley lines, and now it is time to learn about patterns and cycles within the pituitary, the body brain. The way to think of it is as follows:

• Seven years: we experience a complete cycle of body changes.

• Eight years: an emotional cycle is completed and we choose to release or repeat certain issues we may or may not have resolved.

• Nine years: our intellect may change the direction of our interests or introduce new ways of implementation or even take us in a new direction entirely.

• Twelve years: spiritual changes take place and hopefully we evolve in new ways as we break old barriers down and become more tolerant of the ways of others.

This is the period of time it takes for the changes mentioned above to occur, and such a pattern allows the building blocks to develop a strong foundation and equally strong subsequent layers. Each time we transcend and then transmute; when all the cycles are completed together as happens in mid-life we can experience a mini-breakdown that subsequently allows us a significant breakthrough.

Something else we may notice at this time is that we have a lot of cravings, particularly for ice cream or other sweet foods! These feelings are our glands being worked on, perhaps making them sore or swollen, and the way to reduce the cravings or their intensity is by eating regular meals and snacking on sultanas or something similar for the sweetness. A swollen abdomen may occur at this time also, but neither tends to last for more than a few days so don't worry that it's something going wrong – just keep on keeping on.

There are times when the journey will be uncomfortable and we may wonder if it's worth it, but remember how much the rewards outweigh the process – we will be able to serve all others as we were served ourselves and we will live longer and more fully than ever before. Knowing that, can there be anything in the journey that can make it 'not worth it'? The answer is surely no.

Now that we are getting more into the habit of love and trust rather than mistrust and jealousy, we can focus ahead instead of behind. This means that even when we are weary we are making great strides towards our own development and, as a result, in the service of others – love and trust are the only qualities required and we have them in abundance, so we can proceed much more easily and faster than we could before. We will need to remind ourselves of this at every opportunity, especially if we are feeling forlorn or dejected.

As we gain awareness of our presence on the other planes we will begin to feel ourselves projecting straight into higher levels of consciousness. The fourth plane is that of mental activities, and we are in an emotional state to influence others but how will we be received? Will our stability and habitual good humour make us welcome, or will our miserable countenance make others avoid us? What we believe will be perceived and as a result make us a welcome guest or not! Once we reach the higher dimensions, we will reside there as well as here, so to speak. The end result of this for us is everything that happens in our life is a projection, and everything needs to unite in common purpose within us. What this means is our sleep state is one of spirit at night, and soul awareness by day. No longer do we sleepwalk through the day - we are fully present at all times.

A key piece of information to remember is that we only influence events through thought, so our thoughts need to always be positive – so think clearly, logically and positively; with practice this is possible even in negative situations.

We are now in a leadership position – whether we like it or not – and the Management Upstairs can use us to spread the word of the greater discipline. We are like post persons; we visit the main office, collect the messages for those on our round and deliver them as efficiently and quickly as we are able. This means if we feel something strongly we must state it clearly and definitely to be true; if we fail to do so, this will result in others not being able to understand what we are talking about.

This does not always mean blurting things out as and when they come to us; rather, if someone is talking to us and states during the conversation their opinion on, for instance, ghosts, we would simply state our feelings and opinions on ghosts, allowing the person to make up their own ideas. Our job is to communicate the feelings of the higher power, and we can tell by looking at someone's life if they already work under the same conditions as us. If they do, they are under no pressure and are simply making up their own guidelines as they go along using us as a sounding board.

Also at this stage of the process we will be getting through to spiritual levels too, which will be the reason for any disturbed nights' sleep at this time – it's a result of clearing the path ahead, but as we will have broken through the negative side-effects it will enable others to make their way out of situations they are going through which are similar to those we went through in the past. This will give us time for a break, during which we can relax mentally, physically and spiritually, giving to our state of being the chance of having the utmost health and radiance.

There are several levels of higher knowledge, which are:

- Old untruths converted to truth.

- Foolishness converted to wisdom in action.

- Dislike, even old hatred converted to love and compassion.

- Stubborn rebellion converted to goodwill and good humour.

- Complaints and misery converted to joyful living.

- Selfishness and self-indulgence converted to serving arenas entrusted to our care.

- Habitual bad humour being converted to grace and dignity in action.

Once these have been achieved to an acceptable level and we can be trusted not to slip backwards and re-enact old behaviours then we find a new project awaits us. At this time our eyes may be irritated, which is the result of our crown chakra raising its level. That in turn can affect our throat, or perhaps our forehead feels pressured and strained, or the crown of our head feels tender. Although we may be a little confused and wonder what is going on we begin to feel relaxed and encouraged that what is happening is outside our control, so we let go and as a result enable; we may not be quite sure what is enabled, we just know there is no choice now but to let go and let the Management Upstairs manage. Soon enough we will be informed and until then we will just live the day. If you find your sleep is rather disturbed, it is because our ears, eyes and brain are being worked on. Also remember that while a staple of the teaching is to shed old ways when no longer needed, many of our old ways will still suit us in many areas, so don't be worried that we appear have to change everything and seem to take one step forward and immediately catapult two steps back into old ways. Things will even up soon enough.

*

When we sleep we sometimes dream but just maybe we are being helped with changes that are necessary for us to move onwards again. We can experience severe nasal congestion which may mask pain we might otherwise experience. Continuous sneezing on waking can clear this old congestion from our space. We may feel we are moving from one place to another and not be quite sure if we are awake or asleep; when we wake we know something has been going on but we are not sure quite what. These states differ from dreams which in themselves can vary in their purpose. The purpose may be prophetic, instructional, the discharge of old material, a pre-warning of new things and other classifications as well. We need to record these immediately on waking or we forget them. Even a quick trip to the toilet makes us forget, so a notepad and pen beside the bed is essential.

When we experience trouble with learning then a spiritual teacher will be assigned to us by the Management Upstairs. At night we need to go to bed quietly and at a reasonable time. Before we go to sleep we need to think and ask that a teacher comes to us to instruct us. If we persist we learn to be more receptive and, as the saying goes, practice makes perfect! So we can also try to project ourselves somewhere we would really like to be, and see what happens. It can be a real place we have visited or an imaginary place.

Another skill that we need to nurture is listening correctly, because we need to listen to the Management Upstairs as we experience their pressure on us and react to that, so as to cross- reference sounds heard and sights seen. For instance, each ear receives and transmits something different, which means we must listen to one and then the other, alternating between the two to decipher what is being explained to us. The left ear is more sensitive to earth and practical elements, whereas the right ear is more open to the Greater, so using both is paramount. The middle ear hears all, but filters out only what is useful to manifest because the Greater wants us to understand the workings of it first. Picture it like an orchestra: when the musicians are tuning up the sound can be awful, with everyone playing off-key notes and clashing chords, but when they have tuned up and start to play the music is tremendous and powerful. We are tuning up ourselves, but the concert does not start for a while yet, so keep practising; we need to get our instrument in great shape on all levels, and progress is happening at a good pace in spite of what we may think.

For changes to be made in our head we need sleep; these are important changes that will allow us to receive ever-improving audio and visual transmissions. The symptoms of this procedure will mainly be sluggish movement, but as always it will clear and we will regain vitality.

When we are in a state of joy we may well shortly be receiving gifts to make our lives even more joyful, so be of good heart and good cheer. Our time is upon us now, and we are likely to have dreams that reflect this, where we died to the old but the new had to be earned; it cannot just be bestowed upon us. If we have now earned it, we prepare ourselves to be on the receiving end rather than the giving end.

Life now gets more interesting, and we find we are coping extremely well. Natural instincts are all sexually based, in the sense that the masculine action energy is in harmony and union with the feminine reactive energy, and as our sexual energies unite so they develop within us. If we enjoy an active life this will also be mirrored to us externally. This may have been something that has been impossible for some time while the energies were cleansed and cleared of old debris but now we are being encouraged to move into a different ballpark. Now our energy centres are working overtime to attract the correct people to us; at this time we have to release the excesses harmlessly, otherwise the pressure will become too much.

We have, however, been working through a negative energy; it is almost gone now, but our head is so blocked up none of it reaches our higher senses. The positive balance will soon be restored, so try to spend time in a tranquil setting – a walk in the woods would be ideal. Perhaps a sport is preferable, or a good sing through joining a choir, or acting in a dramatic society.

*

One of the biggest queries from the human population as a whole is what is the nature of the more subtle influences within evolvement? Individual religious doctrine aside, greater power is indisputable and is an energy and so subject to disciplines and 'natural laws'. And, just as we do, and indeed everyone else does, guidance can sometimes feel remote and unlovable – but if the law "as above so below" holds water the Greater energy will do as well. The spin-off of this is that all persons working for the Greater, including now ourselves, are subject to mild depression. It manifests itself in various ways and appears at different times, but having reached the point that we have reached, now it is the time for that depression to pass. We will feel better shortly. It's unpleasant, that cannot be denied, but it will go so try not to pay it too much attention. We are progressing quickly and we have come a long way since the beginning – remember, it always feels slow from our standpoint, just as riding in an airplane does not feel like travelling at six hundred miles an hour.

Extended to us from the Management Upstairs is a hand of friendship. Take it. It is a way of showing us some of the magic that remains invisible to most people. Picture a human body – the tip of the head is pointed, a ring where the head would be, a triangle in place of the body, and there is a loop below that. The pointed top is the brain, and the bottom loop is our current energy level – it is actually currently below ground, which is the reason we are unable to feel the Management Upstairs as often as we should, but it will shortly be coming from above again and the balance will be restored once more. We will be raised up, and as this occurs we complete a linked chain that is now finished to make a union of energy with no missing links. Now is the opportune moment to let go and let the Management Upstairs in – all is finished now, there are no more tests, lessons or tears; our life has changed and can be one of laughter and gaiety and happiness, all is new and life from now on will be less difficult than ever before.

When changes to the glands are imminent and under way we will find our nose is blocked, which is to cover the adaptions. That will be the final stage of changes to our body. Although the changes will now be complete, the Management Upstairs will sometimes look at our head during the night; by the time the glands need focusing on the head we should be beginning to feel better than we did previously – our headache will have disappeared, as well as the ache behind the eyes. All that should remain is itchy eyes, and that will be cured with time.

By this point we will be able to use our third eye effectively. The crown is used already so no further structural alteration will be necessary, and once our head has cleared completely we will notice an enormous difference – no one will be able to disguise their true feelings from us anymore, and never again will our light be dimmed or extinguished. They may choose not to communicate their truth but we will 'know' what it is; this causes us to respond in a more empathetic fashion and encourages the person concerned to feel more supported.

It is important that we understand energies and their purpose within the overall plan. Energy is required so that we can motivate others as well as ourselves, and there are places that cater for specific needs in the land mass as well as in people. Sedona, for example, has a multitude of energies available for creation, motivation and regeneration through the mind, permitting a higher work output. This means that, for the people the Greater wants to work together, Sedona is the only place on Earth where they can all be. The eye of Horus is open now, and we can see and hear with amazing clarity as we work for the good of the collection. We listen when we are quiet and we will hear that spiritual consciousness has been added to the gifts we have received from the Management Upstairs.

Avebury in the UK helps us move through the void experience. Carnac in France helps us let go of old aggressive tendencies and find a more tranquil space.

If there was a diagram of our head centres, crown, pituitary, pineal and throat, we would see them linked to the heart, spleen, solar plexus and sacred or base. Each has two halves, the active and the passive, from crown to base. We will no longer learn much from books; instead we will learn most new information from other people. We may come across a wise person who may be male or female, they may hold an elevated position or they may appear quite ordinary. If we are aware we will recognise them from their energetic make up and their interest in us. It is a huge honour to come across such a person. They are usually quite quiet, humble and modest in their demeanour and rarely are they assertive. They will create a space in which we are welcome but they will not insist on our being in it. We may receive a notification but there will be no gilt-edged invitation!

We are a part of the Greater family now. This means we are always able to speak to the people who love and care for us. We're a flower of rare beauty and new energy is within us. They will respect us as we respect them. Don't try to bully these people, nor take more than our share of their time and attention, or we will find them unavailable - as quickly as we found them they will disappear.

We need to be cleared of extraneous information. We have not picked up harmful vibrations; we may not think that, but actually we were exhausted and being tested deliberately. Our surrounding energy field is now more beautiful and it is neither so grey nor so tired. We are losing excess weight and blossoming into the healthiest version of us there has ever been.

Our time has now come. We are complete, and ready to serve as a representative on the Earth. From now on, we are to have no more worries and no more difficulties, as we did in the past; we are a cherished, valued member of staff of the Greater. We are at the peak of the summit and the entire power of Heaven is available for us to utilise and pass into Earth for those evolving to use in the clearance of historical ignorance. We no longer worry about our own personal outcome or that of the town we live in; we just go forward one step at a time. We are being called; we will not be led into false paths. Concentrate on just one thing at a time; after all, we can only speak of one thing at a time so let everything else go for now. We do our best and hope we will be chosen to proceed even farther than the distance we have come so far.

5
A SAFE PASSAGE

All that is past must be put behind us and left in the past. We learn from the past but ultimately leave it where it is, for it is the present and future that matter the most. From now on, all must be newly presented and our material, not from the teams of old. Just as we discard childhood toys and collections as we reach adolescence and adulthood, so too must we now evolve beyond what has come before, taking with us only the essence of our learning to date.

The schedule is being met perfectly, even if we do not understand the process, with no problems in sight. We may be still suffering from a build-up of the past, but that is being cleared – it is now a priority that we shed the past and retain only what is truly needed. Although the past is being cleared, we may still feel apprehensive. Try to take solace in knowing that, despite our anxieties, all is well. We are being reborn, and safely evolving and progressing so well that we are already linked to the next rung of our ladder, even if we are not sure what that may entail.

When the Management Upstairs introduces greater charge into our body, we may find it hard work to adjust and that can have the consequence of sleeping badly. The best way forward is to simply carry on in a quiet, normal, routine manner. Let the Management Upstairs take charge and do what is necessary, and any problems will rectify themselves in the coming days.

Slowly we will begin to understand our revised state of being. Our brain is now one and any symptoms we feel are merely new energies being introduced; the process is almost finished now, but it has to take time because it must be slow. Only a limited amount of sleep is permitted during this time, so we may find ourselves waking early or awake for a couple of hours during the night.

The electricity has already done its job and is now focusing on new people, places and things which are being magnetically attracted to us, so future circumstances will allow us to anchor new energies to the earth. All is now in a state of movement and will enable us to complete another component of our mission on Earth.

By now our crown centre is opening even more, to enable us to be influenced directly from above. It may be that the last time we experienced this was at our birth so we feel very vulnerable. In addition, our consciousness is going to appear cosmic; in other words, our ability to sense will become so advanced that it will be on a scale that we could not previously even imagine. We may find ourselves shedding tears during this process but they are neither tears of anger nor of sadness; they are simply from frustration borne out of our not feeling that our efforts are being noted. But rest assured, they *are* being noted and the Management Upstairs is helping us release old impotence or it would not be happening. If we do what we are asked and work to the best of our ability then our efforts will be noted and impress those working with us from the less visible realms, and we will be rewarded handsomely. By this time we expect no reward and assume nothing, the irony being that we receive more than we ever imagined to be possible.

As the journey is constantly moving, new energy will be introduced to us once again. This may cause us to feel unwell at first, but once it is inside and operating properly we will find a new strength and new abilities that were previously unavailable to us. It is these that have caused the headaches and our feeling unwell, but focus on how much better we will feel once the additions have settled – better than we have ever felt before! Stay strong, find courage, and just keep on keeping on.

We are now able to live a new reality – one in which we have complete and total trust in other dimensions and are certain of our link into and with another set of energies not accepted by many on Earth. As we begin to work into areas of uncertainty we get a new and certain confidence about our ability to see where blocks lie, and so to work at clearing them, so that a turn of the tide occurs and new circumstances step in. When the full moon is imminent a new cycle will have been in bloom for a couple of weeks and now the ark begins to disperse, so be grateful and cheerful, let the Management Upstairs work on us. When the time is right we will be prompted to do what we need to do, and in the meantime, nothing is required from us. It is common knowledge that at the time of the full moon all is magnified so we must remain responsible for our behaviour and not put too great a strain on people or resources that we come into contact with day by day.

*

The Earth plane can appear as a confusing illusion at times, but at some point we realise that love is the bridge to the next dimension – love is a hugely powerful emotion and one that must never be underestimated, it is the universal super glue that holds all things together – but again we will experience the extremes of the energies of both love and hate, light and dark, and then we will step into the next level of light in a state of balance and truth. Having owned both states, that of love and of hate we recognise just how far we can love at this time and that we no longer wish to hate. We forgive the extremes as we find new balance and this now is our jumping-off point. We drop history and forgive it and ourselves, we let go the romantic illusions of what love is and get real in the here and now as we do what we can with what is presented. If we feel the result is passable and we have not deliberately caused trouble or hurt or harmed others then we proceed with care.

We must love our new lifestyle. On most occasions we take baby steps but now and then we make giant strides forward and then we are free of old difficulties. These may present as caring too little or too much but, in either case, we are now able to manage both with relative equanimity. We may be tested for our commitment at this time, which may come in many forms, but we will pass with flying colours – it can easily feel as if we are saturated and we just don't care anymore, but really we care enough not to make things harder for others. We must always remember that anything bad shall pass, and the rewards are worth going through anything, even if it does not feel like that at the time. Remember that and there is no doubt that we will pass the test. We never remember that good things pass in a flash, only that things we judge not so good take ages to work with. We will subsequently rest, and then be able to earth the increased spiritual awareness. We will not feel as ill as we have done previously, and this is because we will now be more fully conscious; and the bridge between us and the higher dimension where the Management Upstairs resides is completed. We will have other negative feelings though, such as headaches and sore gums, which are the consequences of our blood vessels being enlarged to return the cleansing blood through the heart and to the head quicker than it could travel previously. This allows us to take the increasing charge from above safely. We will also be more susceptible to change in temperature – because we work at making communication possible we have a lower body temperature than many other people and will feel cold easier than others. Take a combination of vitamins A and C and get some rest.

We are like a flower in bud – our stem is strong and healthy, our roots are good and deep, and our colour is white with pink tips and brown roots. All is well, so keep on keeping on.

Our head may be hurting because the Management Upstairs has been carrying out the final adjustments to ensure the new pattern is established beyond any possibility of mishap, and this meant changing the pattern. However, the new pattern is enacted, so we are fully integrated and in a permanent state of meditation now. We can go anywhere at any time and no harm will befall us, but we must always return to a natural phenomenon to recharge. This can be woods, a garden, a park or even a tree, just somewhere to be at one with nature so we can re-centre at a core level and link to the highest again with the help of the Earth as well as the invisible realms.

Something we should be aware of, and no doubt pleased with, is that we are never alone anymore. No longer just an individual, we are guided by the Management Upstairs. We are just now starting an adventure in which we have a major part – management of our role is taken care of by the Management Upstairs. We are like the ugly duckling that became a swan, and the swim is going to be magnificent.

*

Our anatomy harbours little-known secrets of the body and the world we inhabit. On the left hand, the little finger showing a way of getting our own way is arising. The fourth finger represents a wedding of the polarities being made possible by uniting the male and female energy to create the possibility of a third force. The longest finger, the middle finger, is the pointer to instinctive action stored in the historical memory, while the first finger is the pointer for the next logical step. The thumb indicates the foundation of loyalties within the third dimension.

On the right hand, the little finger is the time to think of a new foundation and to bring in the invisible world. The fourth finger displays the new devotion that now lies beyond existing manifestation. The middle finger gives the chance of mind control as opposed to brain repetition. The first finger indicates that a new way of observing should be pursued, and the thumb shows that if courage is shown it will be magnified a thousand-fold by the Management Upstairs.

For the feet, the left foot's little toe indicates the grounding to third-dimensional zones. The fourth displays an example of the extension of Earth energies. The third toe is in sympathy with the element of water, the second is in sympathy with the element of fire, and the long toe with the air or ether.

On the right foot, the little toe shows the link to the mineral kingdom. The fourth toe shows the link to the plant kingdom. The third toe shows the link to the animal kingdom, the second to the third-dimension composite, or the human, while the big toe indicates the ability to pass over into the fourth-dimensional zones with ease.

Of course, this is only a basic guide but it is interesting nonetheless and it is the opportunity to incorporate symbolism in a personal way and make sense of it.

Another way of working is about to be earthed and will reach all dimensions. A flower of great beauty will then radiate from the world. It has been said before and it will be said again: many are called but few are chosen, and those that are chosen are utilised to the full. We have been chosen, to continue to evolve, therefore we will be utilised to the full. From age to youth we learn to communicate on all levels, up and down, and communicate with the higher worlds more effectively as and when we make the effort.

There is a time of many changes approaching. Our organs are a different shape from what they once were because they all now serve the Higher, and have been adjusted to the needs of the Management Upstairs rather than those of the sensory worlds. We will be losing unnecessary weight, but do not be alarmed. Just act sensibly, drink less coffee and tea and more water. Our neck may be stiff for a couple of days, but all we need to do is get good sleep for the next few nights – rest will restore our energy and get us back to normal. Good and faithful service is the sign of a new beginning, and this time it will be a better one than ever before.

We were taught in the higher dimensions and this now has to be translated in a relevant way to as many other people as possible, so they can learn from our wisdom. In order for this to happen our own life circumstances need to be radically altered to give us the freedom to move about as invited and as is necessary. This will allow the information we observed to come back to the universal mind to be reorganised and applied according to the needs of those who can progress the evolvement of the new age. Our physical and emotional testing is over; we are completed for now, but not yet mentally activated.

The Management Upstairs needs our discipline and cooperation just as we need its grace and love. It is grateful for the dedication and commitment we are displaying, so keep moving forward, content with the knowledge that we are doing well and pleasing all.

If we notice an increased craving for sweet things do not worry. It is simply a result of the endocrine glands secreting the hormones needed by the brain to allow revised gene activities. Our own central energy is to be regenerated and switched on again, because we finished a section of work and we are spiritually tired but we are recovering now, just craving sweetness temporarily. Remember, godliness is love, and to give is a godly act.

An eagle flies high but sees all life as accurately as though it was on the ground watching something a mere two feet away. That represents our development now, as we are able to see so much in many dimensions. A flower symbolises good odour as it is pollinated and so a new sexual energy is created and is moved on as it creates the stimulus to move things forward again. We are progressing in many ways – apart from what has already been explained, our understanding has gone from strength to strength and continues to improve daily. However, we are going through the negatives, and these will be transmuted as we see more clearly, hear the instructions better and know the way forward, so don't worry. Negatives can, and often are, used to help, rather than being something to be fought against.

We are now part of the team of the Management Upstairs and we are able to work as a mediator on the earth as well as being a meditator so we act between the dimensions. We will become known as a communicator and will be the esoteric go-between, so our own development will start to expand and new dimensions will start to open up for us in the service of the earth. But don't worry about feeling out of your depth or being daunted by new prospects, as instructions will be continuous. It has been said before and it will be said again now: many are called, but few are chosen. We were called and chosen. We walked through the maize true and free although with compounded difficulties; we are like the plant that breaks the surface and heads for the stars, and as our roots are solid we are more able to fly free. The tests are behind us for now, so take some time to rest for a short while and then work in areas that will give you enjoyment and where you are invited. Flying free is an effort and we have made a tremendous effort, so we need to recover and do things at a less fevered pitch.

Our health is excellent, but there are changes being made in our harmonics that mean we will feel awkward, but as always this will pass. Neck pain experienced at this time will be tiredness caused by depletion; some gentle stretching should help to alleviate the aching. Our glands are fine, but discomfort there is the result of the bloodstream carrying the energy around the system as fear is released, but again, put up with it because it will soon pass. Love is upstairs and down, that's a fact, and our role will be to demonstrate this love in action by showing new ways to cope in situations where adjustments are necessary.

However, all the beauty and promise of our life going forward must come at a cost, and that is the discomfort we will feel occasionally as we get to the next point. It is like climbing a mountain where we move from base camp to base 1. At these moments in time, we may feel vulnerable and probably quite bewildered, and probably also dizzy and nauseous. This is because our head is being cleared out, and that can make us feel quite off and incapable of doing what seems to be required of us. We have no choice but to get out of our own way, do it anyway and hope for the best. Of course it is being done through us and not by us, but we have to do it many times to believe and trust that this is so. We may experience headaches and discomfort in our eyes, and this is a result of the new ley system as we carry electric and magnetic forces not yet familiar to us. The crown chakra is extremely sensitive and at this time we are subject to fluctuations in our body as well as the effect of adjusting to the ley, or guidance systems of the Earth and the stars, so until the resonance is detectable we can experience discomfort. This will pass when the new system is safely in operation, but until then do not become too pressured, and if you do then take time to reconnect with nature. But just as a glove is a servant of a hand and our body is the much-loved servant of the spirit so we will get all support, help and encouragement that it is possible to give us.

Although we live today in a society of equality for the genders, it must not be forgotten that men and women are different from each other, and not just in the level of our hormones or our reproductive materials, but also in the internal energies. For instance, the female energy present in both sexes is the four flower principles – love, purity, truthfulness, faith. We are now about to attract the composite form in another person because we have faced them all within ourselves. Now it is a choice if we complement

43

another, for we have enabled a union with ourselves. A large tree trunk shares a common truth with a sapling tree trunk: it is made up of particles of atomic structures that need no advice on how to live. They know from the highest level, and we do too, so feel a reverence for yourself and care for your temple. The Management Upstairs is a living state, and we are their representative here on the Earth.

As the Management Upstairs influence our pineal gland, that influence passes to the pituitary to enable us to make the required changes in the body it can feel as if our cranium feels enlarged. The cerebellum, or dragon brain, has released more information into our space and we have to upgrade, update and accommodate this, to make use of what is required now. Eventually this will permit us to use all information immediately instead of having to assess through procedures, as we currently do.

By now, the fourth dimension is an area of which we are very knowledgeable. The small piece that is still at work on the third dimension is only a tiny representation of the whole, so any time we think that we are limited and doing only a little, take a break. Review all you have learned in your time on Earth. Multiply that by twelve, a spiritual turn of the spiral, then multiply the result by sixteen, the corner points of the physical, emotional, intellectual and spiritual frameworks, and that number is the equivalent of our knowledge at the higher dimensions. Remember, though, old habits die hard, and establishing a new one is threatening. Therefore, our level of courage must match our energy level – if our energy level is subject to fluctuation through pressure then we will slip back and reinforce the old habits, so be careful of this. The saying "act in haste, repent at leisure" comes to mind, so make each step meaningful and ensure we are all as ready as we can be, to continue on to the best of our ability.

*

Now let's talk a little about the seasons of the year, as it's important we understand them. An approaching winter may seem like a welcome release from a long year in one half of the hemisphere. It is a time where we can stay in, read books, listen to music or whatever we do to rest up. During quieter times some may feel old ghosts are returning to taunt them, old indigestible issues may be tasted, or perhaps heard and seen one final time before being cast aside forever. It is a useful time and enables us to free ourselves.

Spring will take us into new avenues and will permit an ongoing, permanent state of freshness and newness to arise. We hope for better things as new life buds into being. We reconnect to the sacredness of new life and find respect for the Earth as well as for the less visible realms of being. We begin to look forward rather than back once again. This is not only for the nature kingdoms but also within us, and for every single person working for the Management Upstairs, the reason being that light is needed in areas of shadow more than it is required than at any other point during the year.

The ability to work within such areas requires us to be apprenticed with people who possess more experience than we do initially while we lack the ability to see the big picture as clearly as they do at present. It is confusing when the mosaic of nature begins to take shape and is connected to the light. We will need to be sensitive enough to follow the clues in order to solve the mystery in time; also to have a level of street wisdom, which then connects to others working into other areas of light, so the seasons within us become less severe even if in the community they are horrendous. Even so, we better appreciate the beauty that abounds year by year.

The season of summer provides an opportunity to enjoy, to get together with others and to give joy to others, and to receive. There appears to be a level of isolation. All of this is, of course, music to the ears of the laws of nature and is of enormous benefit to the densest levels. Whatever we do - sing, dance, swim, pursue sports, eat together or whatever - we give and mirror back with joy the gifts we gain from the Earth as well as those we receive from the invisible realms throughout the year.

Autumn is when we offer the accumulated wealth that has accrued not only from us, but from the family around us that comprises our working environment throughout our communities. As the harvest is gathered in, we have the time to have a harvest celebration with family and friends before considering future policies and planning. We spend time with colleagues, comparing notes and getting any advice needed before making hard and fast decisions. We might even decide to go away for a couple of days for a change of scene.

Why all the talk about seasons of the year? Because all of us go through a version of the annual cycle each and every day, with the particular season we are experiencing being a little more exaggerated than the others. As we become more aware of ourselves we are more able to be courteous towards others as we recognise more easily where they are in their cycles of being. This also encourages us to be able to discipline or quell the inevitable storms that take place within and without! Eventually we are able to be relatively calm and so supportive most of the time. We may be there but we will be considered supportive if, as a result, all benefit.

Checklist:

- In what sort of situation do you find your buttons get pressed?
- Are you able to take time to consider and so to react in a responsible manner without a loss of temper?
- How much do you believe you are able to trust yourself to behave harmlessly towards all?
- Can you accept others have the right to their beliefs and the space they are in, as you have a right to your own, and agree to differ if need be?
- Which season of the annual cycle do you consider to be your weakest area and how do you support it to enable a strengthening within?

6
LET'S GET ON WITH IT

Overshadowing can take place through a being who is involved in more than we are, from a realm beyond our understanding. Our personal overshadowing takes place when we are in need of information beyond our current capacity to impart, yet deemed necessary by the assembled group. We remain in our body but our cellular structure is used for a great being to use as a malleable stone-like substance that acts as the foundation, on which it can temporarily rest. We are not being taken over; it simply means we stand back and enable another to be at the forefront. Initially, we recall nothing and feel absent in the astral realms, one of the reasons to be well trained as it is not at all helpful if we collect things we do not wish to bring back with us. If we want to attract the more advanced beings it is logical that we must be disciplined and clean to be able to attract them.

This requires a changing of our atomic structure, so we feel as if our bones are under pressure. They are, of course, not used to this state any more than we are, so react to the change. As they are the densest foundational level of our being we have to wait for them to catch up with what is already a fact at other levels. As we acquire more subtle abilities, we begin to understand the problems of our changing atomic structures. One symptom, for example a sore throat, illustrates our search for a new means of expression. When gifted with one it brings new problems because we don't know how to handle or use the gift and we can feel frustrated and impotent as a result. Where once we imagined seeing angelic forces, we now realise that this is rarely so.

As the levels of awareness are passed, many environmental factors intrude and they are now always necessary in the current situation. Therefore, it becomes extremely important to work only within the needs of the moment and to allow old patterns to be released into many space particles. So, cleansing is carried out with the aid of white light, ultraviolet and royal blue, within the controlled atmosphere of the Greater's colour room. The cleansing is not an overnight task, though when through the first stages we emit a new sound which then has to find a revised form.

*

The Management Upstairs is in a state of growth, dependent on the appreciation of existent knowledge. Knowing that, we cherish the information that we are granted. Definitions play a tremendous part in understanding, so learning how words can be applied can make a big difference in communicating effectively and pleasantly with a broader range of people. Remember that we steer the car, but the Management Upstairs drives it. We can be anywhere and if the Management Upstairs requires us to undertake a job then we will be moved where required to complete it, sometimes without knowing why or what we are doing. So, we are free to visit any destination we wish, for a vacation or another reason, but, just as a doctor is on call, if we are needed elsewhere then we will be moved on accordingly. How we are moved on depends on the situation; we will not receive a telegram, postcard or phone call, obviously, and instead a scenario will play out that results in our moving on. For example, we may have a minor car accident to release us from the place we are in – but there's nothing to worry about. We probably may not even be hurt and the accident does not need to be serious, it will just be a means to an end. If we take notice when our attention is drawn in minor ways there is no need for a major incident. If we do not, then the signs and symptoms will become progressively more extreme until our attention is drawn and we take notice.

For as long as we are here on the planet it is still necessary for us to experience and learn and we only realise our growth with hindsight, rather than being informed and thus able to use foresight. This is because if we look forward rather than back we risk not fulfilling our job description. Back views take us to the back. Forward views project a future that may or may not occur, dependent on us and others who surround us. Our limited self was content to continue, and the Management Upstairs had to break through the natural reserve of fight or flight to get through. We must understand the gift of the presence and be there paying attention.

We are in a state of change – that much is true and undeniable. We are changing dimensions, not classes, and so you are experiencing changes in your temperature, as well as experiencing body turbulence and weight gain. This is like being put into a foreign and alien environment at a new place of learning with people you do not know. It is a culture shock to be overcome as quickly as we can adjust to the new stage. These things will settle after a few lunar cycles, at which point we will be able to fast and the excess weight will fall off as quickly as it piled on. Adjustment will be automatic but will not be immediately forthcoming; we must wait a little while for it as we earn our passage. This is the usual method as it is both quick and efficient, and it is known to be safe. Certainly there are things we can do to force growth, but we will not be ready for it and the people we need to contact will not necessarily be available.

A snowflake is a cellular structure, were it turned and described north to south or, put another way, from spirit to nature. From east to west, start to completion, we experience the circumstances or framework within which movement is possible. Put them all together and we have a chapter of movement; from north to south, or above/below, then we will see that when you work through the life circumstance of that arena the experiences are sifted and shifted until they become as one and fulfil community needs seamlessly, with no staccato jerks. This in its sophisticated form becomes economy in action. It just is, with no pain or strain, and others accept it or they don't.

The Greater can be considered the best new age scientist of the light. It is pleased to be able to speak to us, because we are now one of its representatives, with the gift of being able to serve and communicate on its behalf. The mission is to prepare us and others to be able to use sensory skills of a lighter order – not necessarily through meditation, but rather a light in action regardless of the skill remit being extended. This is because our sensory skills are being heightened and it is the Greater causing us to feel bloated, sick, achy and under pressure, and this is the result of our being treated to such a degree that we become inoculated and immune, so we can keep on keeping on without any further problems in the future. If we are called on to work with others we must be 100% accurate as we relay messages, otherwise our usual level may not understand. We must trust the Management Upstairs to know what they are doing even when we do not. We must pass on instructions or helpful tips in spite of apprehensions that we will be laughed out of court. Only through practice and constant repetition will we no longer question but trust unconditionally.

Our first aid kit is primarily our mouth, and we must continue to be available to advise, in order to establish basic disciplines, because occupying the mind with trivial, but necessary, everyday needs really serves to divert it from panic. So we answer questions as best we are able, and suggest work projects to buy the time for all to settle. When this becomes possible, and sometimes it will take years, we are happy to be made redundant. The student has passed the teacher and all celebrate as they choose to re-associate in a revised form or to go their separate ways. It is the implosion of consciousness and natural growth that is causing the mind to question and look without; for guidance, implosion means that with non-conscious choice the information is available and unless disciplined guidelines are imposed from outside, experiences will overload the vehicle and it will self-destruct. But we will have no trouble in relating to this, and our understanding will increase as we are instructed and guided from within. In just one short year we will be able to extend well beyond our years, and we will have a wise head even if it is on young shoulders. So remember, our natural reaction will be to think others see what we see, but they do not, they see what they see. Remain aware and never disregard the young, as they may be the message carrier, and take notice of the seniors who remain lively and active. Be curious: how do they do it? They are certainly not a part of the living dead masses, so they have something of use for us, but they will not share it until or unless we ask. This is why it is important, as mentioned earlier, to understand different definitions and interpretations, as this will permit us to speak more capably to more people, fluently, passionately, calmly and persuasively. Think how much easier everyday life is by talking the same language as the people you wish to communicate with, and when we can appreciate how important it is to speak properly and clearly to others, especially those we are trying to influence, it becomes fulfilling and immensely satisfying. The ability to speak and hear is often taken for granted, but if we stop to think for a moment about communication in other ways, it is easy to see how blessed we are. As one example, if you try to talk to a deaf person, either they must be able to accurately lip-read or we must utilise sign language, otherwise the words must be written down. If we try to converse with a mute person, we can hear each other, but you will both need to be fluent in sign language or, alternatively, communication will need to take place through writing. If a person is deaf and mute then our only option is braille. So we can see that the ability to talk and hear makes communication infinitely easier, and from there we should see the importance of relating to other people's viewpoints and definitions of words, as that will make the easiest form of communication even more effective, minimising the risk of being misinterpreted or inadvertently offending someone. Even if someone speaks a different language and comes from a different culture, our whole body can message their whole body and they are able to pick up our message without a word being spoken. It may not be as precise or as accurate but they will certainly be prompted to ask us questions that they need answering. If we are able to do this without their being 'weirded' out we are moving from amateur status to that of a professional.

We may be granted the gift of sight and sound, because we have used our gift of touch wisely and shown responsibility and maturity in its use. We have grown into it carefully and steadily, so we will also use the other gifts to provide direction to others, particularly those who have direct influence over various parts of the population. People will seek us out, and they will not be conscripted or coerced; they will want to find us, and it will be a relief to them when they succeed.

Great and blessed are those who are humble and meek, as they shall enable others to inherit the Earth. We are working to become such a person, if we are under the influence of one of the greats who organise and arrange future planning for us all. We need to be obedient and willing to administer our time and our gifts in any way we are able to contribute to holism and eliminate division. Those above whose influence we work with will be in agreement about our own powers, abilities and integrity. Our path is now becoming clearly defined; we have progressed sufficiently well, and, accordingly, those who are to work with us are being pulled in and put into place, while those who will not work with us are being given exit permits to be removed out of line, thanked and freed to move on to work with others.

If we consider ourselves to be in a vertical partnership with the Management Upstairs, we are the junior partner, but we are a partner. Yes, we may be expected to do the majority of the donkey work while the senior partner appears to be absent. But, we only have to call or to be in trouble and the senior partner is there in a flash. There can only be cooperation between the parties if we commit ourselves with integrity of purpose and a desire to evolve, as this creates the Management Upstairs' ability to move and overshadow us. There is thus an interlock situation and everyone benefits from it. Despite it being in everyone's best interests, it is a cosmic law that the Management Upstairs cannot move in until invited – if they moved uninvited, our freedom of choice would be overridden and over-written and the wrath of the guardians of the light would be incurred. It must a cooperative partnership, not a dictatorship with us as the oppressed, and therefore our full permission is required at every step of the way. Any arrogance will have to be eliminated for it bullies rather than suggests. Superiority must give way to true care and concern. We are involved in freeing others, not in stitching them up. Nor are we using or abusing another, we are encouraging them to achieve their full potential. If they have skills which are different from ours, that is fine and we may be able to cooperate; if not, that is also fine. Neither must we feel used or abused. If it were a dictatorial situation, nothing would be achieved and a lot of effort would be expended without its ever bearing fruit. This contravenes the law of economy, so to create an efficient organ is complicated. As complicated as it may be, it is possible and also we must find boundaries so as not to over-extend ourselves or others as necessary – as we are now an organ, the Management Upstairs is able to streamline to put us to work on their behalf, to utilize our abilities to their maximum potential.

Checklist:

- What do we need at a physical level? A massage, a trip to the gym, a treatment? Decide and action.

- How do you feel? What would you enjoy that is a real possibility, a trip to the movies, a visit to a relative or friend, a manicure, some time out? Establish and action without guilt.

- Do you feel understood? What could help, a phone call to a friend, a trip to a counsellor, more information, a course of study or something else entirely? Work it out and take the necessary steps.

- When did you last visit a holy place near to you and where is it? A park, an open space, a church atmosphere, a lecture or talk or advice from a wise counsellor, be they priest or shaman, tribal chief or someone who has a proven track record in your community. Make the appointment!

- From answering the four queries above make a plan without attachment to a result and make the first move.

7

THE CHAOS WITHIN THE GHOST HUNT

Inside ourselves is our true reality, while outside our body we receive experiences and input that may influence us to a greater or lesser degree. All that is spiritual, and our soul helps to instruct and guide so we are able to work out what is relevant to us and what belongs to others. We try to unite inner and outer and we practise until we are able to harmonise one with the other. The sacred union is when the heaven is in our body on the earth. We eventually find ourselves unable to live a lie and become true to ourselves, hopefully without giving offence or harming any other creature as best we are able. "As above so below" is the enabler that motivates us onward and maybe upwards within the evolutionary journey. At each stage at a certain unspecified point the vibrations which influence us can change, sometimes radically; maybe through illness, relationship change, job relocations or any number of other circumstances that appear to be beyond our control. Suddenly there is discord until life is sifted through and we extract what is relevant for us and make a real plan that it is possible to follow step by step. It can be a long period of servicing before we reach a harmonious state. It is bad enough within our own life, but when it involves families, companies and communities as well it requires a clear head that is able to focus, clear debris and accept or reject with equanimity. Work to establish and frame, or create a boundary around, a project, and then work on the piece of the puzzle we are on, knowing that otherwise we will not make headway in solving our mystery. All this with a good heart; it takes trust and courage to move forward and for progress to be made, we are essentially ghost hunting – clearing away the past, letting go of what's holding us back. As a result, the old shadows jump out at us before they go; only if we can accept that and rise above old limitations are we able to stand free in the now, free from the past and ready for the future, really centred in the gift that is the present. All this in spite of our fears! We need no longer be shackled by it. It is almost like being resurrected from the dead. The new birth that propels us onwards can be from our own perception of what is required, or may come from another person, place or project. One thing for certain is that it will not be anticipated or expected and will carry a shock element. This can be pleasant, for it carries an element that enthuses; it does not need negative association - that is a part of old historical ignorance, material from another person, stored within the walls of a building or contact with places that were foreign to us until now.

As a result of these incidents in our life, the chakras must work in pairs in order to plough through old fears, so we are able to decide what action to take and how to react as a result. This takes time and demands both time and space so we can consider options to enable a cleansing of all that is now out of date and just getting in the way – similar to old, unused files taking up space on our computers or in our filing cabinets; occasionally we will have a rummage through to streamline and release some space. The new, instigated through meditation, prayer or contemplation on our lives, maybe even spontaneously, must now be worked within our life. We have a mystery and now we begin the work of servicing it until we find a satisfactory outcome. We start with cleaning up the energy centres within the body. Then we sift through the varying levels of the energy fields that surround us; the aura, as it is often referred to, lightens and we are ready to move forward once more. Unlike doing some spring cleaning, though, it can cause us to be sick or experience skin problems; the good news, though, is that we can help control this by breathing. A fast first breath is expressing our willingness to breathe in and take the help the Management Upstairs are offering us, usually in spite of the conclusions we made of the past regarding old learning and its consequences, not to mention our behaviour! So we breathe quietly and we take time to enable a more gracious outlook within us and a more cheer-filled countenance.

The 'boy' within us accepts the new adventure and presents the masculine action energy, which is the bearer of new standards and learning, and can be considered by the Father who applies wisdom in practice. All is under the direction of the Management Upstairs. The 'girl' explores a means of being held secure yet examining the varying presentations: representations of the Earth, Mother and just how much she can get away with without incurring wrath or disapproval. The discipline of Mother Nature shows how we can organise and administer the new regime but still fit into the greater picture accommodating other projects and people. All must now be updated and upgraded so that the abstract and the actual, the male and female, go hand-in-hand, walking in the same direction, with the same goals, rather than clashing and fighting.

In varying disciplines 'rules' of service have a seven-year period of cleansing, during which time sex takes an internal, rather than external, form. The body is made sacred and the mind trained, after which normal service resumes. Unfortunately, though, some disciplines misunderstood this – hence sexual depravity! The saying "give me a child until seven years have passed and they will be mine for life" comes to mind. This training is not supposed to be a forever thing. After a requisite period we are more able to serve both the heaven and the earth.

If all this occurs under the guidance of a wise mystic they will help us balance the spleen with the purpose of cleansing the core of being. This results in health, balance, and a secure platform that serves as a strong foundation, from which we can move on once again. There is a positive outcome from this: the expression of life will change. The throat and the voice open and deepen, both in agreement over the policy update. If we are unsure of how well we have done, interactions with others often test our progress, as our partners mirror our strengths and weaknesses back to us. This isn't an encouragement to be promiscuous, though, and need not be sexual!

Once all of that is out of the way, the heart's duty is to love without an expectation of a return. It is love for love's sake, rather than calculating what benefits we will get from the process. To love is to give your body and your mind, not either/or. Old shock, like confrontation or narrowly avoiding being hit by a moving car, is stored in the high chest. Disappointments and disillusionments are stored in the mid chest, and the low chest stores our feelings of resentment towards God or nature for seemingly having hurt us as we learned. Eventually, though, we take responsibility again and establish a smoother rhythm, free of the pain of learning. Now we surf the waves, so to speak, rather than seeking the thrill of the peaks and the slough of despond of the trough. Although we do not give much thought to learning, considering it just something that happens, it's worth remembering that it is always frustrating and often painful, because it challenges us – learning a new instrument or self-defence challenges us physically, while studying quantum physics or a new language challenges us mentally. Either way, the point is that we are challenged and it is painful, but once we work out how to process the information we form a rhythm and take the knowledge for granted. Learning has always been difficult, but we manage it – we can speak a language, read, write, drive cars, operate technology, so never shy away from anything because it has a learning curve. We must dramatise to feel and here too we can underplay or overplay - it is up to us.

If our third eye is clear enough to gain vision and the Management Upstairs rubber-stamps it, then the energies join via the crown, before going to the back of the head and the shoulders while we protest loud and long, or we become a martyr to our own suffering! Not a guarantee for popularity! Then we begin to grow up and abandon the tantrums, sulks and protests, knowing that the Management Upstairs does not listen to the spoiled brat – it turns the volume down on us, giving us the silent treatment, until what we ask for is far less selfish and more 'grown up' in nature. What we want is to truly explore the potential of creativity in action, to understand Heaven on Earth and release others from fear so all start to vibrate to the sound from the heavens in accordance with the needs of the Earth and to balance the systems so that they present a foundation for the next stage of work. To those who give unselfishly in the service of others, without taking over or disempowering, more is given. To those who take, the learning becomes harder.

The Earth's gravity field must be harmonious with that of the Spiritual directive, and the Earth's field or shield must be able to bear its share of the pain of the natural releases occurring both in people and in natural fields. Just take a look at the weather patterns and natural erosion to get a level of understanding of this. As we get selected for use we will be close to many people who are going through personal initiations, and our role here will be acting as a communicator, facilitator and mediator. This is a state of reception and transmission. Our training for this has been completed to a required standard, so we are now safe and stable within the updated dimension. We have been proven to a standard that we have already been tested against.

Our energies are flowing well and any aches or pains in our hips and shoulders, elbows and knees that we experienced until now will be cleared perfectly, as if there was never anything wrong with them. Our next area of work will be revealed and make known to us shortly. We are likely to feel lonely around this point, and that will be the consequence of separation from the godhead as well as a phase of familiarity on the Earth – this will be fixed before we know it. Know that all is well, enjoy what you are able to enjoy and commit to research of new areas that are of interest.

Sometimes in life the negatives just get to us too much and we feel bogged down, unable to continue for fear of further hurt. It is important to never let the negatives weigh you down, but instead to keep pushing forward, finding the ample positives all around us. Yes, some things close off but others open up if we take the trouble to look for them. Accordingly, our solar plexus will be adjusted and be made safe from old negative experiences, associated with birth or the start of new life. This will allow our heart to open and the love we have collected and stored in the heart can now start to flow and spread to others without condition.

Despite all the positivity we are now experiencing, we must still go through some changes; nothing too strenuous, but not as pleasant as if everything was perfect. We may notice a rash on our legs or in other areas of our body, which is to allow stored toxins to be released from our body; also, our glandular system needs to realign because our third eye is expanding, so do not be surprised if we experience a sore throat or aching in our neck for a few days. Just give ourselves time and space, forgive misadministration, whether our own or another's, and 'do the day' quietly and this too will pass! Now our nervous systems must re-align and settle into new and calmer association.

*

Let's talk about regression for a short while. No doubt you are familiar with the concept of past-life regression, whereby we can be hypnotised and recollect memories from a previous life. This phenomenon can happen spontaneously when we meet a person we have not met before but we 'know' them through and through. We may visit another culture or place 'we know' yet we have not consciously been there before.

Many people like to think they were kings, queens and other noble members of society, although the truth is the chimney sweeps and murderers also had to go somewhere! Although often mocked and rejected by many over the years, regression has become almost acceptable, although not yet respectable, and it certainly makes for an interesting academic discussion. What aren't so often considered, though, are the feelings and entanglements that could ensue should this fascinating possibility emerge within the personal realm of experience.

Consider this hypothetical scenario. We are enjoying the romanticised idea that we were a North American Indian in a past life – a mental picture that is appealing to many – and everything that goes with it: the natural life, being so close to Mother Earth, and so on. But what if the child to come through you in this life was in that past life a character who was instrumental in your death? Not necessarily (although possibly) directly responsible, for instance as your murderer, but maybe generating hatred towards you, or setting off a series of events that led to your demise, or by your being ill and this person wilfully neglecting you, or even causing you harm that resulted in your taking your own life. You might not become consciously aware of it, unless you had undergone past-life regression, but perhaps unconsciously behaviours were questionable. So the question is, can the past and the present, or future, be reconciled in behaviour that is acceptable in the present, or will the memories prove to be too disruptive to handle and all revert to ancient history?

Or, imagine this: you are the parent of a stubborn, rebellious and inert child, despite your having done your utmost to help the child and provide it with positive opportunities in life. You go for a past-life regression session and discover that your child tortured you in a life in New Mexico, during the time when the Spanish Conquistadors overpowered the existing lives and encouraged decadence. Your child is the person who challenged your origins, tortured you because they could, and made you suffer. Armed with that knowledge in the present, would you provide deferred justice and make that child suffer for their crimes in a past life, or do you overcome the karmic debt to free yourself and your child?

The mind does of course play tricks, but it also expands and it is all too easy to confuse the two – but then, does it really matter? Because whatever the reason is, when you experience it, that experience is real enough for you and it must therefore be handled appropriately, rather than dismissed as a "trick". Until that time, we can exercise our free choice with responsibility, rather than rushing in where angels fear to tread. We also need to be mindful of whom we trust. No doubt there are many, many incredibly knowledgeable therapists – in both the orthodox and alternative camps – and full credit must be given to them for both their insight and dedication to care for others, including their quality control upon Earth. However, there are others who, like the backstreet abortionist, mean well in their actions and genuinely want to help others – indeed, who think their actions are the best course of action for people – but their limitations and ignorance often add to the load of others rather than reducing it. It is therefore a prime concern that we seek and use only the very best people we come across, and not just trust any who say they are capable – a mistake in that decision can be very costly indeed. If what someone does has little or no effect, or they appear to be trying too hard to impress, they probably are not the person for us. We need to keep looking until we 'know'; with practice, we will.

In many ways the stress and strain of modern life is greater than it has been at any point in history. This is not to disregard the troubles of people during wars or times of discontent, but it is a simple acknowledgement of the way life works today. The speed of life increases in a linear pattern with improvements in technology. The Internet and portable communication devices like smartphones and tablets mean that connecting is globally possible and individuals are contactable at any point in the day rather than standard office hours – making it very hard to relax with the family or even enjoy a meal out in peace. Thanks to technology like Skype and FaceTime people are able to have a video call with others in any corner of the globe. The world is a small place now; travelling from England to America is no longer a two-week boat ride but a seven-hour plane ride, during which time passengers can watch the latest blockbuster, enjoy a hot meal and have a powernap before landing. The end result is that we have more possibilities and opportunities than at any point in human history – but it comes at a price: a big concern today is the carbon footprint we are leaving from the burning of fossil fuels and the impact this is having on the environment. It is as much of a concern that this is only part of the problem; our increasing usage of transportation and digital devices has led to a dramatic increase in toxicity within the human, animal, vegetable and mineral kingdoms. We find ourselves in a peculiar place; we have the opportunity to harmonise and lovingly bond to humankind at all levels, while also trying to protect our bodies from the assault of pollution on multiple levels.

A question to be asked is: is this challenge helped by every person being allowed to do their 'own thing', as our recent liberal society permits, or in any family, including a societal one, must we learn to work together to a common denominator of what is best for all? Regression is not for those who are not yet ready to be responsible within their capacity to communicate – just because an idea has consumed them it does not mean that they can inflict this passion on others; rather, it permits them to gently probe and suggest, but then they must wait to see whether or not the idea is picked up. But the decision must be independent, not forced one way or the other. Sometimes people can see what is best for other people but the person in question cannot; in such an instance it is tempting to persuade or push them in the 'right' direction, but this can lead to more harm than good – many people will instinctively rebel out of principle, even if they actually want to go in the direction in which they are being pushed.

People all progress at different speeds, some are ahead of us, some are level with us and some are behind us. Whatever we do, we must not make the mistake of getting arrogant or acting as superior to another while progressing, or dominate or be aggressive in any way, shape or form. That compounds old victimisation through dictatorship, just what we are trying to 'ghostbust' We must all work within the framework of all the other people involved, so we have to refrain from trying to force something before it is the time when all have been made ready. They have come from a different background, with different influences, including, perhaps, ethnicity, culture, religion and other doctrines. All of these shape us into the people we become and shedding the shackles that bind us is more difficult or time consuming for some people than it is for others.

Regression is growth in its own way, and growth is a natural state, not one that should be inflicted upon us. Parents do not order their children to get taller or develop mentally, those things happen when their biology dictates. Being irresponsible can make the pressure too much to bear, so really the best support is to simply mirror back what has been said, even if that's just a practical basic suggestion, but never volunteer, or worse, insist, that we are right or wrong because really we have no idea – we, like everyone else, are working within the limitation of our personal experiences. Given that life is a subjective experience, there can be no absolutes. Yes, we have books which are already a point of reference from the past and as such considered a rough guide. We have people who have proved their values in service and those who just say they have!

Only when we become as one with the invisible and the visible will our company and knowledge be sought by some; our centre point is located in our navel, our upper arms are the heart and throat, while our lower arms are our spleen and base. All must be equal before discomfort is eliminated. Others who may shun us or be shunned by us have a different set of circumstances to standardise, not better or worse, just different. Bless them and leave them to it and expect the same courtesy in return.

The need is great and our release has been completed. Our task has been to rid ourselves of our past, because that is what has made us into a tough nut to crack. It was useful at the time, but is now superfluous to requirements. We had a crash course of "I want, I must have, and preferably at your expense" to allow us to be compassionate rather than critical, because that is what we were; underneath the charm offensive were self-indulgence and self-interest. We either break down this ghost into small critical fragments and work them one by one as we repeat old patterns, or we unite with the holy, release old architects' plans and create new ones. As we do so, we become more flexible and cooperative with others in our team. Between us, we create a thing of wonder, one that is required on the Earth by the Heavens as we are over-lighted and blessed in our endeavours. The leg is releasing through cramps the demands of the past as it is reflected in the present. When we state what we want we will receive what is possible – but only in the form of what is appropriate to our karmic process; if we want everything then we want too much and will be unable to process it. Think for a while and then write down what you think you want. If this is too difficult to do, write what you know you definitely do not want. Here is an example of what your list could look like; some of these entries may inspire you, and it is acceptable to add them to your own list:

- Someone to provide me with unconditional love. Someone who is free, someone accepting who does not concern themself with age or the scars of life. Someone I admire and respect and who returns the same reflection to me, so we can love and support one another, while free to pursue our own areas of interest as well as sharing others together.

- An abundance of both income and lifestyle so that we can support others, in generous and beautiful surroundings.

- A shared workload, so that no one is exploited or overloaded yet each does what they do.

- To be sufficiently free to do the Management Upstairs' work as and where required.

- To love, like and care for youngsters who have the courage to bridge visible and invisible realities and to say so. To give them a platform and points of reference as required.

- To continue acquiring knowledge, and learning to develop my own gifts as I activate each one. Then to pass the practical ways of supporting this on to others.

- To work with the invisible world in a state of joy, harmony and contentment on Earth.

- To release and forgive my past with love and gratitude to all, and to not stand in the way of anyone else's evolution or hurt them in any other way.

- To be involved in research into the invisible and to get to know my teachers.

The energetic chakras are an integral part of each one of us and as we learn to use them they gift us happiness, growth and release:

Base: When, for whatever reason, the bottom falls out of our world we are left with no option but to reorganise ourselves so that we can carry on again – especially when we come to the realisation that no one else is going to do it for us, it's down to us! This may cause us to feel impotent or frustrated, but until and unless we try it, nothing will change, which means no more progress and that we are just harbouring useless information within us. Yes, we may feel vulnerable, but have another go, you have nothing to lose and everything to gain. After all, universal guidelines state nothing is added to our doing nothing, so we have to keep going. Once we have a go, though, whatever we have done can be rearranged, added to, re-routed and so on. In short, a little adjustment gives us much space in which to work.

Sacrum: If a meal is no longer on a menu we will not still try to eat it, and the same is true in life – we must get over it and move on, not dwell on how things used to be. Just like a drawer or a wardrobe the centre will get full, but there is only so much space in the energy fields. If it is cluttered up with things acquired in the past then there will be no room to accommodate the new things we have picked up. So, a spring clean is in order – we throw items away, give them to friends or charity or sell them, thus providing more space in which we can put our new items. It is a nice idea, in theory, to get the new things before discarding the old, but unfortunately it doesn't work that way; the old must be discarded first, thus creating the vacuum that nature will abhor. If we do not do this, then we rot, causing everyone to be unhappy. We are not able to go back in time or insure against loss; the truth is, old clothes go out of fashion, cease to fit or look tatty, and the only safe passage is moving on again and letting others do the same.

Solar Plexus: Rethink and rework, we serve the apprenticeship the long way as we start to learn our trade. It is only when we do that that we can afford to start taking short cuts and still produce the results that are required but we must learn the correct foundational levels first. If we do not have self-worth or self-confidence then we may need much external validation and exposure in order to be able to begin the new propaganda while at the same time trusting ourselves to still remain modest and display humility.

If it has previously been a big struggle then it might be a difficult area each time, so we will need encouragement in order to move forward.

Heart: It is a necessary requisite to attempt to understand how much personal work or meditation is required at different times so that the rhythm is maintained. To raise the standards internally then personal work, meditation or even deep retreat are all needed, and just as we get used to that and start to like it, we are sent into a period of internal service to whoever enters our domain, for as long as required. The meditation period itself is relatively quick, the service continues for as long as the rhythm is required on Earth and then back to the drawing board we go, awaiting the next step. As soon as our will aligns with that of the Greater, new rhythms are established and both the internal and external unite in common purpose as they deepen yet again. At that moment, we feel comfortable – during the transitions we can feel uncomfortable, and although we don't like it, it's just a part of the transition process that we must deal with. We must also trust in what as yet remains unknown to us, and it is essential that we accept that the old way is not working or required any longer and we must let go of anything that has been trying to control us.

Throat: Once we understand, we can think of how best to express ourselves within the updating scenario. If we are too busy to see individuals then we must instead do group work. We follow traits and trends instead of being divas – we are grateful to use any tool or means that makes our lives easier! As a result of telling our truths we may end up rattling others' cages, so we need to learn how to look after ourselves instead of hoping or expecting others will do it for us. We must release our "be perfect" self-driver in favour of what works well enough. It is tempting to try to attempt the administration of both Heaven and Earth but of course neither is in need of a management consultant, and even if they did they may well opt for someone else anyway!

Third Eye: Old dogma must be released because methods that were effective or utilised in the past may not work now, in the same way that floppy discs are no longer relevant in our world of CDs and cloud storage, or cassettes are of no use in the digital world. Time moves on and things change with it, and rather than having major peaks and troughs we learn to surf the waves we encounter with equanimity. We are more detached, more discerning and have far less criticism of both ourselves and others. We are pleased to do our bit and are grateful to others for doing theirs, and with combined efforts we are content to be serving a greater need much more effectively. It is at this time that we may leave old teams and join up with new ones.

Crown: As we let go our need to control or manipulate anything and are content for the Management Upstairs to manage we can finally relax. When we receive our summons we work to the best of our ability, sure that what we have to offer will be of an acceptable standard, and that it is our state of being that does the work as we and The Management Upstairs work together, as well as on our own account. We handle ourselves with flexibility and ease whatever the situation, regardless of our age or stage of progress. We know that we have been broken down and deformed and the reformation is a work in progress. Top down to base, the new impulse has come from the Heavens, and base back up to top we have responded and now the new circuit is in place and all is well. It is therefore time for the new to be activated, so we wait patiently to be shown what to do, where to be and how to do whatever is next. Then, as we test the new circuit we discover that all things are indeed new and efficient as well as being effective in spite of us, even if we claim it is because of us!!

We will be pleased to know the update and the upgrade of all that was old and worn is proceeding just fine and no fasting is necessary to facilitate it now. Gentle exercise is recommended though, as is plenty of sleep – other than that, let the Management Upstairs take control!

It is never nice, and indeed can cause rampant insecurity, when some people in a group use others as currency. There is no glory to be had by loudly proclaiming any work that you are doing, and even less so if the work is being done for the sole purpose of gaining credit from others. Remember that anyone being used is very likely being persecuted rather than cherished and cared for. Looking after others is incredibly important and one of the main purposes of life, so never neglect that duty in favour of trying to impress others or using or abusing yourself or another.

This journey is all about giving permission so that change can occur; it occurs by placing trust in the highest invisible ideal that form can be given to, then creating a warm, nurturing space that is safe, and one in which old patterns can be released.

Doing so will mean making an effort to always, whenever possible, work to a compromise that is mutually beneficial, rather than helping one while hindering the other party. It also means actively looking at the needs of others, especially those who have been attracted to come to you for help. We may think we are sensitive, but do not assume that we instinctively know what others need without giving them the courtesy of letting them explain their situation to you. Neglecting this simple lesson means not giving credence to mind and body, and if we are not prepared to give respect and courtesy then the individuals going through difficulties who have sought us out may very well be better off without our help.

Let's take a moment to look at our individual traits of mental, emotional and physical predisposition.

Mental: We have a good mind and can be incredibly intuitive and this allows us to influence others. We have the capacity to understand the needs of others. We give and serve without a selfish thought, but we can also take life too seriously; make sure we spare time to allow ourselves some fun. We are a searcher after truth – we have a need to find the meaning and purpose of life.

Emotional: We can give to the detriment of ourselves. We always have an open house and we love both animals and children. We value possessions, and we care about people. We like to help people feel at ease and we are comfortable around others, partly because we are highly sensitive. However, it's important that we don't take life too seriously. Our moods change quickly, so we need to love what we do – there is a requirement that we use our creativity, and this will bring us joy. We are sentimental and often possessive, but we also know what it means to love unconditionally. We have learned many of life's lessons the hard way, but the upshot is that we can now help many other people. We need space but simultaneously have a lot of love to give to a special someone. Ultimately, we have a lot of potential and creativity, so use it.

Physical: We are creative, so use that creativity – failure to do so will mean we stagnate and become extremely unhappy. We are sensitive and could benefit from more strength, so use a gym, train, do exercise; we are perfectionists, which does not help our sensitivity because criticism is not taken particularly well, nor should it be given. We are very driven and many things interest us, so we must use our creativity to beautify our surroundings. We can be self-centred, but not always deliberately; rather, it is usually just from a lack of awareness. We are sociable and outgoing by nature, which will be mirrored by the importance of physical activity in whatever form.

Spiritual: We must allow the wisdom inside us to express itself. We have a strong will, so pray for the Will of the Greater to be done through us and we will realise that it is being done through practice - we will be shown how to do this. Our life will be dedicated to helping others; and we will have purpose and be aware of the deeper meaning of life, so we must follow our star. We have a need for loving relationships around us, and we also require harmony and peace. Our mind is very good but we need wisdom in our affairs, so as to stand up and be counted. Another of our requirements is the feeling that others love us.

We are now clear of the past and able to live in the present, but that doesn't mean we are the best we can be. In order to empower ourselves it is necessary to know our limitations, and that can only happen if we are 'roughed up' somewhat. It is a privilege, joy and blessing to work for the invisible world at a profound and elevated level – so do not take it for granted – but on Earth it can seem more like a curse than a blessing sometimes. Souls in bodies can be extremely arrogant, because they question their own beliefs by using us as a psychic punch bag. Remember that faith is a fragile state at the beginning of its stirrings in people, so people worry when they examine their fears and resentments and too easily project them onto us. We have to learn to toughen up in a new way. Within the body, pain teaches direction; in the mind, fear teaches definition of space; in the spirit, anger teaches us use of energy in time. The ultimate sacrifice is continuance. It is imperative to release the despair that can come with success, because success guards loneliness and prevents interaction through service. Release the luxury of failure too, because failure buys attention through freeloading, which negates self-validation; too often we are just not ready to manage the demands and projections directed toward us by others. To court fame brings another set of new problems and we have already discussed power used unwisely. We must be trained to manage the energies and know how to stay centred regardless of all else.

As we accept who and what we are now and how we fit in the grand scheme of things, we find and keep our personal identify, an essential skill as it is where we meet others at ground level. When that establishes itself it is safe for the Management Upstairs to work through us knowing that the energies will be directed as they wish them to be. Not all people merge as one unique defined drop of the ocean in love, in light and in the truth of expanded awareness. These states must be worked on and earned in each step of the journey. Within us, this puts calm abundance and joy where once there was pain and grief.

*

Our efforts and understanding take us forward at a pace we can keep up with as our understanding grows. We feel more stable and physically we are able to catch up with the required adjustments in the various body systems. As we change and are changed we must adjust honestly, handle the pain involved, and then be as accepting as we are able to be. Our relationship changing within ourselves also affects those around us, so we must allow them to adjust to our changed state. If the future has in store for us peace, joy, serenity and popularity in measures that we have never in our lives experienced before, we must go through several gateways that control our exposure to them.

The upstairs/down balance is as it should be and we will be shown how to proceed from this point on. The Management Upstairs will have stood back to allow us to release the sacrifices necessary for the work ahead, but is now ready to proceed again.

We are transforming into an agent of healing who will work and live in the most gracious of manners, and our self-understanding increases with each passing second. We have overcome the subconscious resistances and all is well again. This marks the completion of this stage in our training; our bodies are all fit and many can contact us as and when they desire. The Management Upstairs will show us the way and make the opportunities available for us; all we have to do is complete the work we started and know that all is well. By this point it is important we stop judging ourselves as harshly as we usually do – our thoughts are pure and full of care and concern for others, so take comfort in that and know that mistakes are normal.

Checklist:

- Who or what from the past keeps coming into your conscious thoughts?
- Who needs to be forgiven, or who do you need to be forgiven by, before you both can be blessed on your way?
- What do you need to let go of so you are in a space where new things can enter in?
- Are you in a space where you can welcome what comes, even when there is a basic plan within which you are flexible?
- Can you still your body and mind at will, so keeping centred on the earth and open to the heavens at all times?

8
AS ABOVE SO BELOW – THE HUMAN CONDITION

Are we able to balance our core belief with the feelings of incompetence that we harbour? Is it within our capabilities to understand the reasons why we feel trapped within situations that we consider to be unfair? Is our mind whirling and our body anxious? Are we restless and impatient? Are we sensing changes are coming and are wondering what to do about them, the likelihood being that we are becoming more self-aware?

Meditation is an art form that, over time and with repeated practice, calms the mind.

Relaxation is a gentle discipline that is applied to the body to release stored anxiety.

Contemplation helps us to hold the new revised vision while learning to cleanse each component part one by one, so as to optimise performance day by day until the two merge as one and become a living state.

Say the following aloud:

I choose to forgive the judgments placed on me by myself and by others, in particular by those I love, be they parents, partners or children. I no longer wish to be condemned, outcast, abandoned, rejected, stoned, discussed, poisoned, picked at, persecuted, sacrificed, abused or ill-treated, nor do I choose to be affected by superiority, arrogance or judgments of those with less compassion, tolerance, patience or competitive and jealous behaviour that divides and separates through hatred. I choose love and lightness of heart and mind. I forgive others the pain they have caused me and I forgive myself for believing the verdict of those I care for, for understanding their viewpoint, for feeling inferior and so allowing them their spoils of war, and having an attitude that accepted those whose fortunes were experiencing a tough and rough phase. I choose to keep a caring, tolerant and inclusive manner, but also to cleanse myself of the anguish and pain through which I learned and was taught. I pass it to my soul, mind and body, and I thank them for helping me to become who I really am as I reconnect to source.

The light and love of the Management Upstairs are in my life and for all members of my family. I intend that all be free to enjoy the fruits of my labours and have no doubt that all will do exactly their own work in their turn without my backlog being added to their own remit of work. We all have a busy schedule planned for us and there is much that depends on our will to serve and our good understanding, so we need to stay dedicated and focussed.

Our body and mind will become as one and our pathway towards love is widening. Light fills our space and our future is one of love, service, joy and care. Our family is free and full of vitality; even though each has their individual pathway, the old collective is freed of debris. As a result our body's memory banks are being sifted and cleansed, so we are able to work without our negatively affecting others. The pathway is established and our colleagues are now subservient to the Management Upstairs while also being respectful of us. All is well.

At this stage of our journey it is good to take some time to reflect and answer some questions. Set aside some time, perhaps after a walk to clear our head or a relaxing bath, when we are in a good state of mind and will remain undisturbed; do not, however, wait until you are going to bed, because then our mind will be tired and ready to switch off – we need to be relaxed but still engaged. When we have the right time, outlook and place, answer the following questions appropriately and honestly:

- Do you think that you are leading things forward by yourself, or are you feeling somewhat bemused or like a runaway train?
- Are you going to be willing to do the mechanics of jobs without expecting anyone else to do the nitty-gritty, such as reading the map to get somewhere or checking the restaurant reservation?
- When others do that, do you appreciate their input or resent their interference?
- Are you willing to convert what you have found out to a simple and sequential form that others can understand in spite of their challenge of both it and you?
- Are you willing to keep meticulous records, which you will file and can later refer to when necessary?
- Are you willing to collect information and then document it in such a way that others may challenge it but you can justify your actions without feeling resentful?
- If you try to get your viewpoint over to others, are you willing to be patient and loving, repeating yourself in varying presentations year in and year out, without letting yourself be bullied by those you are supporting?
- As a result of the role you have been placed within, are you willing to take your position without victimising others because of it, yet still feeling able to get the job done?
- As you lead others within your particular skills area, do you betray the trust placed in you through disloyal behaviour to yourself, your family and colleagues?
- Can you be flexible enough to allow others to practise their skills without having to be dominant?
- Are you able to be humble enough to go where you are required without losing your balance or running away?
- Are you modest enough to be able to join in whatever is going on without having to change the routines of others or play a starring role?
- Can you obey your inner guidance without disturbing or disrupting others around you, or interfering in things that are not your primary concern?
- Are you feeling calm and patient, willing to 'be' and are you able to

'do' only that which is required of you at this time? If not, explain why.

- Are you relaxed about the situations you find yourself involved in and are you willing to give all your best shot because you are grateful to be involved within any service?
- Do you give others the courtesy of your truth when asked, or do you try to conceal it? Be as detailed as possible in your answer.
- Can you present your truth to yourself or to others in a civil manner without losing your temper, sulking, shouting or bursting into tears?

Although it may be difficult, try not to feel too let down or abused by those that you placed in positions of trust and who exploited that position, through dishonour, bad intent or making you disillusioned by their methods or desire to oust you or take your role. Like many others, you are hurt by the cruelty you observe around the world and the unkindness within inter-relationships may shock you. These are sad things, and the negative emotions we feel as a result are part of being human. Do not grant these people such power as to dictate how you feel; you must take a reasonably stoic stance and push forward, making positive changes as you go. They in their turn will learn what you already know, so leave them be.

Checklist:

- Make a short precis of where you think you are right now.

- Ask the Management Upstairs to illustrate through everyday living if they agree. Look for three illustrations through sight, sound or experience and be observant of things or people who attract your attention.
- Think what appears possible as a next step.
- If you really do not know, then involve yourself in the day, having informed the Management Upstairs of your findings to date; now we are willing to be patient as the Earth Mother leads you step by step.

- Consciously work for peace and stillness within, regardless of external distractions.

9

A WILLING SERVER REGROUPS

We have experienced, and felt, many negatives in our past – resentment, greed, control, manipulation – and in order to be released from each one they have been reactivated. At a certain stage they rear their ugly heads just once more to enable you to be absolutely certain that we are free of old ways of being once and for all. When we start working within ourselves it is painful enough. As we make progress we start work within our family grouping. If we are successful there we are gifted a community project and so move onwards. If we hope to emulate such great peacemakers and we begin to research their lives we observe most of them spent a long time in isolation of one sort or another. It may have been in prayer, playing or composing music, meditating in a sacred temple or whatever brings one to an altered state. When a service period comes to a natural conclusion and we have to pass our old responsibilities on to others we may feel somewhat at a loss. We wonder if we have done our old job well enough and if those who learned with or through us are up to the job they are to take over. Letting go and getting out of our own way, not to mention the way of others, requires us to trust and accept the chapter is ending even if the book has not. Getting off our own case and out of our own way is a key factor. Not to mention getting out of the way of others concerned! They will not necessarily have the same experiences as we did. We have been released; now we go away to lick our wounds, rest and recover, prior to returning in the fullness of time.

We will have suffered discomfort as a result of others taking liberties with our gifts, our quintessence, our compassion, our patience and our willingness to serve. As their toxins are placed into our space – our body, home or car – we need to find relief or the space to regenerate as we may have become saturated. Repeat the following aloud as many times as you feel is required:

I choose to free my body from all sickness and stay focussed, keeping my mind on the light, peace and warmth on Earth. I ask to feel safe and to have a cosy home, in which joy, peace, love, light and common standards and objectives are the norm. I ask for this along with the health and glow of body, which makes me an anchor and a convincing message when out and about. I ask to regain direct contact so I know it, and to be able to serve you the way you want me to, how you want me to and where you want me to, but the stable foundation is a must to keep me anchored and earthed. Thank you. Your humble servant (your name).

Our new life awaits us; there is no action that is required from us and we simply need to deepen our level of trust, acceptance and the knowledge that our abilities are to be used to their maximum capacity in a different format. We have been taken apart, worn parts renewed and cleansed and now we are being put together again in a manner suitable to age and stage. Then we will try various scenarios out in arenas that are required on the earth at this time.

There is a truth in life, which is: the behaviour of all reflects on the one, and the behaviour of one contributes to the whole structure. We must choose to accept, trust and surrender to the union of the Heaven, the Earth, the past and future, the limited and the free, the soul and the ego, the heart and the head, the mind and the body, the invisible and the tangible, the doing and the being, the male and the female, the active and the passive, the old and the young, the same and the different, forever. Only when there is union and balance can the fire of love introduce us into the new. In yogic practice this is the kundalini rising. When we are ready this phenomenon will occur; if we force it ahead of time it may be very difficult to resolve life issues that surround us. This is the time that the saying "when the student is ready the teacher appears" becomes a truism. Someone here on the earth who has been through similar circumstances in their time will be present to us. No fuss, no fanfare, no beating of drums, and often no special recognisable clothing, so we need to be aware enough to be able to 'feel' their atmosphere and their state of being. Such people will recognise others working on a standard harmonious to their own in the wink of an eye, others may not. They will certainly not advertise, they may be recommended, or alternatively we will just come across them seemingly by chance. Usually quiet, often shy and quite happy to be alone, they are easy to disregard if we are not maintaining our awareness and watchfulness. They carry quietude - peace and calm. It surrounds them and permeates all. They are good-humoured and unattached to a result. The invitation is there, take it or leave it. That is up to each one. If the opportunity is missed it may be a while before we get another chance, and the person who presents next may not carry quite such an elevated stance as the last facilitator. So it is better for all if our awareness is kept constant.

Fusion between spirit and matter requires that we are able to love more unconditionally than we did before, so frustration and impotence convert and becomes a willingness to be flexible during hardship or testing times. Impotence gives way to compromise in the interests of a collective; anger gives way to being motivated enough to hold a higher standard than ever before; fear gives way to the ability to have the courage to care; grief gives way to being more compassionate and empathetic than ever before; arrogance gives way to humility and a non-expectation of input from others; and cruelty gives way to gratitude as one's assumptions prove to be without foundation and history is rewritten in a new form. We celebrate safe in the knowledge the foundation established will be strong enough for a building to be erected. We may not be certain what it will look like or how it will come out when finished, but a new excitement begins to creep in, in spite of ourselves. The cynicism gives way to new hope and renewal of interest in service, however it may occur.

This results in reformation, as a union between doing and being, active and passive, demands that we live to the same standard of acceptance that we have provided for others in past times. So, if we have loved and cared for others then we need to be accepted and acceptable, and this will demand that we live to that standard ourselves. Only at this time does a regrouping start to occur. We may find some people we know just appear to dematerialize and others just appear! We just observe and maintain our lack of attachment to a projected outcome. We are OK if we do 'hang out' with those people, just as we are all right if we don't. We just wait to be shown. Of course, if some of the people we like are from the past and they have proved their value and worth in their own right, we celebrate. It is reasonable to believe that the new people coming in will have the skills and the standards of those who are 'keepers' from our past groupings.

If people wish to stay and live in the past, they will feel guilty about not suffering; for as long as they think they should suffer in the interest of someone else whom they care about, at a certain point this will no longer be tolerated and decisions will be made in spite of us not because of us. If they live in the future, they can hope that others will soon arrive at the same point they believe they have reached, but are they right? Perhaps they will become so disillusioned with waiting in their ivory tower in solitary splendour that they become detached from any reality in which others would be able to reach them. If that state goes on too long, then medical intervention will be necessary.

If we live in the present then that which we have depressed within us will be able to find a revised form of expression. There are so many illusions as to what people thought they were entitled to, as their right, in the marketplace at this time, and their appeal must begin to be dissolved. Each of us must maintain our ability to discern those whose energy field matches and is married to their skill remit. If they do not think it matches, then their search must continue until it does. Compatibility is essential, arrogance and superiority is not; it is a fine line but one we must walk.

We all make mistakes - that is how we learn. Accept the mistake, know it has taught and tempered us and move on with a firm step. Alternatively choose to be disillusioned and hide away or welcome the newfound vulnerability as an excuse not to live as fully as we might have been able to otherwise. People can choose to feel insecure and dredge it up time and again instead of finding their new place. Certainly we fumble around somewhat, as we acknowledge disappointment, even disillusionment. We have taken so much time to learn to apply and contribute to a community in a responsible manner, and to serve others, we have lost our joy and the ability to demonstrate our state, so we must give time and space to be regenerated and replenished in a new way.

The chaos, confusion and bewilderment as people begin to untangle another facet of the collective mystery requires patience, and to honour everyone as much as possible. No one is betrayed if we are truthful in stating our needs and we are never disloyal if we work to free ourselves from areas that have caused us hurt; we never harm others if we care enough to free them to face their destiny, rather than try to control theirs as well as our own. We do not need to be nasty, but we do need to be truthful if we are to ever communicate accurately. Everyone loves other people, but it's impossible to know the permutation of skills required to do another's job, and that is why they are present and start at the age they do, just because they have no idea. So trust them to know, and trust the preparation they have had to give them the required ability to face their task. If another will not let us be who we are, then keep quiet and absent ourselves. If not, it is a hiding to nothing; the other person is so fond of their own voice and their own philosophy they will not listen, let alone hear - that is not communication, it is domination. If we have no wish to subscribe to that regime, we must get out of the way and establish something more conducive to us and others elsewhere. Trust in the greater power and that the Management Upstairs knows what is required by all and what we are sensing but do not fully understand, any more than the other parties in the exchange do. We accept as graciously as we are able our part as things move forward with as much dignity as we can muster; knowing that we have done our best throughout and now we can stop trying as we let go and let the Management Upstairs show us our updated identity and the role that has been created for us to play next. We work with cooperation, in harmony and in the belief that all are being served and the best interests of all parties are being met. We let the light guide us, love infill and surround us, and goodwill warm us as we are purified and flexible enough to bring joy into our life and our service of and on the Earth.

Checklist:

- What aspects are no longer working in your life?
- What no longer holds any interest?
- Which family members or friends are apparently no longer available to us?
- Which areas and people are you drawn to visit?
- What do they have that you would like to experience more?

10
THE NEXT STEP IS THROUGH FIRE

When our progress is strong, we sometimes need affirmations to remind us of our task and our responsibilities. Using the voice reminds us of the expressions we wish to use, in the same way the different types of yoga use breath, chanting and physical mobility exercises, as do many other disciplines. With that in mind, we can repeat out loud any of the following that have relevance at this time:

- I want to nurture and not exile.

- I want to cherish and not banish.

- I want to hold all around me secure and not isolate any.

- I want to love and not selfishly demand.

- I want to hold safe and not conquer.

- I want to support and not dictate.

- I want to encourage and not tyrannise.

- I want to free my partner, parents, children and grandchildren to live in peace in the way they want to.

- I want to unite a standard of behaviour, a code of ethics and a working hypothesis with a reality that honours each and every one, so their individual skills and talents are given full expression but the collective is flexible and solid, and the centre pure. This will mean all who need to drink from it are regenerated, refreshed and rested when they are fully laden, and those who have suppressed their anger, fear, pain, frustration or impatience can find the courage to keep on keeping on until they find an avenue of expression that satisfies their soul without harming anyone else.

- I will erect boundaries that drink in the cup of life as I learn not to take in intellectual, emotional or physical ills that are not mine to experience.

- I will discriminate and be discerning with abstracts projected by others, only taking in those that are relevant to me.

- I will take time to look at preconceptions, misconceptions and misjudgements that come to my attention, regardless of whether their source is me or another.

- As the process of evolution is accepted and trusted I undertake to release harmlessly the material not required by me.

There is a desire by people to be harmless, and this makes it easy to judge others as being inadequate and then put them down and even disregard them. In an effort to avoid hurting people and be sensitive to the needs of others, we cannot stand accused of not caring for people, or abandoning or rejecting them. To do so goes against the core teaching of our journey, where we are to do the exact opposite – to care for people equally and unconditionally, and recognise that everyone has intrinsic value. However, what we may find is that in our effort to be kind we are accused of being cruel, demanding or expecting too much, too soon, too often – these are criticisms to take on board as we can adjust how we act, but ultimately it comes from wanting the best for people and trying to encourage them to reach their full potential. In our willingness to honour and be tolerant of a need to experience directly, we can feel that others batter us with their own projections. We may feel we are being bullied by others in their effort to prove that their opinion of us is correct; they may even victimise us to try to ease their own despair. That is bad enough if they do it on their own behalf; when they claim to be doing it on behalf of another then it feels like mob violence. When lip service is paid to one thing but the language of the heart or the body indicates something else, all we can do is to absent ourselves. We may take a retreat, or even live as a partial hermit for a while.

We must remain constant and secure when criticised or condemned. There are some people that just cannot be pleased – if we do act, we do it wrong; if we do not act, we are neglectful. After such responses it is easy to feel dejected and unloved, but we are strong, important and needed. Stand up tall and repeat the following loud and clear, with purpose and pride:

Bruised, battered, beaten, tired and in pain I stand naked before all. I forgive and surrender. I do not want to be resentful, sad, fearful or angry, and I hate no one. I cannot be grieved or terrified anymore, I cannot do any better, nor can I act any differently. I cannot prove that I care, but I do. And so with this knowledge I let go and let in the Management Upstairs. I leave be and place my trust in them. I accept things are as they are, but I know I love. The Earth Mother knows that too and will demonstrate it to me through life circumstances. I will wait patiently in this holy space until that time comes.

The hardest part of any task is the beginning – whether it's an essay, a public lecture or a marathon, it is always daunting to start. That is when the nerves make themselves known, the doubt creeps in with the reminder that "you still have time to back out, you know; it isn't too late." To start work that involves a dimension alien to most people gives rise to repressed fears, sadness and frustration, as there emerges the niggling curiosity, the negativity that ponders whether you are capable of withstanding the impending challenge and all that it brings. But fear not, because as we are now, the answer is "Yes". Not "Yes, you can just about make it through if you push yourself", but a resounding "Yes!" that has no doubt about it whatsoever. Holding our standards while others seek their own requires potential and courage; both these are developing and being tempered until just like fine steel we reach the stage of tensile strength – flexible, durable and capable of wounding; the testing for this tolerance is exactly what this whole journey of ours has been about. In the process of our progression we have managed to reach a level higher than was anticipated at the outset, so congratulations are in order.

There are certain rules of thumb in life that we should be aware of, and it is also our duty to make other people aware of them when appropriate and without suffocating them. They are:

1. That which does not honour, destroys.

2. Anything that does not defend, attacks.

3. If it is not gentle, it is violent.

4. If it is not filled with peaceful intent, it is a continuance of war.

5. Anything that does not bless, curses.

6. Anything that does not tolerate, humiliates.

7. Anything that does not love breeds hatred.

8. Anything that does not lighten exposes darkness.

9. That which is not generous is mean.

10. If it is not shared, it is selfish.

11. If it is not kind, it is cruel.

12. To see wrong living in oneself is difficult; to see it in a family is to have reflected ancestral pain; to see it in a community is horrendous.

13. That which has been built up must be broken down before transformation can be possible.

14. Through fire it becomes possible for a life to be transfigured according to the purpose of the soul.

The new day is dawning now, and it takes us towards the new age of peace and joy. Walking through the fire of old issues must be undertaken prior to new life starting. Many are fearful of death and letting go, others find the anticipation of the new too threatening. As a result they opt to repeat the familiar rather than release it and allow their life to be made new.

Checklist:

- Pick the issues above that draw your attention.
- Try to work out their source.
- Choose to forgive yourself, even if you do not know how.
- Choose to forgive all others involved.
- Ask the Management Upstairs to sort it out on your behalf, as you know you cannot judge or assess what is required.

11
TO LOVE IS TO FREE

One of the hardest parts of life is accepting that it can be difficult. Brutal, even. From being bullied in primary school to not being part of the clique in secondary school, then trying to get along at work – if we are lucky enough to get hired – all takes an emotional toil. These things can cause depression, a lack of motivation, insecurity, anger, jealousy and many more problems. The saddest part of all is that everyone feels as though they are on the receiving end of some injustice, even those intentionally dishing it out to others – if people acknowledged that fact, there would be less suffering passed on. Nonetheless, as life is not so simple or ideal for that to be the case, all that is left is to accept that that is the way it is and overcome it – which is done by continuing to push forward, not letting it grind us down, realising that we are better than others are giving us credit for and the harsh words are not realities about us but internal grief being displayed externally by people suffering their own turmoil.

So, we must learn to stop lashing out; such behaviour makes us a part of the problem rather than the solution, it makes us violent rather than gentle and it makes us engage in war rather than try to find peace. If we do not want to be any of those negatives, we want to be the positive counterparts and let go of all the times we have been on the receiving end of a lashing. Otherwise, these will only fester inside us and will create feelings of resentment that we need to overcome so as to be able to love all equally, rather than dwelling on the past and what it has served up to us.

Relinquish the bad feelings of being shunned, being ostracised or made to feel insecure. Similarly, release the memories of the times we were the one doing the ostracising, by being aggressive, selfish, egotistical or hostile, even if we felt the reasons were justified – the end result was making another human being feel lowly or worthless. Reflect on these misgivings, take note of how those actions were mistakes, and let them go so we can serve modestly and humbly, in peace, filled with joy and cooperation, collaborating with life as it is managed by the gods.

We are a child of Earth, Heaven and etheric reality. No one would know from talking to us that we are an instrument of the stars and under instruction; yet, whether they know it or not, everyone is affected by that truth, including us, so trust the Management Upstairs to show us the way. Do this most appropriately by accepting what comes your way, and knowing that you are free to love and be loved. The rest of God's children need your skills, so, to use a biblical phrase, "go forth and multiply". We spread our knowledge and skills to all who will listen willingly. We are at this point being prepared for our new work, but don't worry about still being unaware – we are not to find it, for it will find us when the time is right.

Sometimes people encounter the power of the Heavens, to such a degree that they feel dominated and feel that a gesture is necessary to showcase the distress being experienced. Divorce can be an example of this; although often it is just the separation of a married couple, it can be much more – a gesture to make sure there are rewards in a manner that ensures safe passage. This gesture can bring up deeper problems in relationships, with a husband, wife, child, parents or even peers. Sometimes people want to monopolise others to convince themselves that they feel important or necessary, or simply because guarantees are wanted. Yet in life all people, all places and all things are only on loan. People own nothing; life is but a fleeting moment of time, a slice so thin that it would be completely invisible if one looked at the Earth's history on a timeline. That puts into perspective human arrogance and cockiness – people do not inhabit the planet for long, and need to realise that. Everything is on loan, but if things are stewarded properly the lessons that are learned can never be taken away. Unlike the removal of possessions, this is not a punishment but simply removing the danger of plateauing out, as that can only lead to disappointment and unhappiness – people are on Earth to grow as souls, not to learn some things and then have a permanent rest.

So, growth is important, there can be no denying that, but it is also important to grow appropriately. That may sound strange – after all, surely the only way to grow is up, like a flower? In a way, that is true, but human beings are complex; we have been gifted the most incredible mind imaginable, capable of learning so many things throughout our life. That mind is like a muscle – it needs to be exercised; if we neglect our muscles they will at best stay the same size and strength, but there is the high possibility that they will get smaller and weaker. A neglected mind will similarly wilt, so there is a need to remain stimulated. However, growing appropriately means observing a broad range of topics, and this will make our growth far superior. If a person prefers one direction over all others they can experience breathlessness, heartache or the desire to return to the ideal of divine love, rather than struggle, negotiate and interact with misunderstanding. Alternatively, there may be a feeling of being dragged down by gravity, and experiencing an Earth atmosphere that can cause disturbances in the pelvis as well as aching legs and feet. Subjectively, this can be interpreted as a form of despair as well as disgust at observed behavioural traits throughout history, e.g. hostility, aggression or illness. This could be due to fatigue and exhaustion, because habit forces people to repeat patterns that are no longer appropriate to their age or stage. Ultimately, people have intelligence and creativity in abundance, and it is criminal to neglect that power.

To release the feeling of being pushed around or not being equal to others in the emotional, intellectual or physical life allows people to revise, review and update, prior to making the decision on whether to repeat the actions or release the past and try something new. We need to provide time and space for the soul to get back on track and realign us with something new, fresh and stimulating. If we do not take the time to adjust and give space to both ourselves and others, through meditation, prayer and contemplation, we could be forced into a space where we will learn to gain immunity from the dramas of others, without having to come into direct physical contact. This means when we do come into contact with them we do so without interfering with their growth, by being overprotective or caring too much. There are dangers, both visible and invisible, from vicarious existence. Whether it is a safe passage through the psychic or not, though, the regulations remain the same. The love granted from the divine enables the individual to be cleansed by fire, which is electric and instantaneous.

Compassion for all works more by friction, which is uncomfortable yet necessary for collective care and development. There will be times when we feel that we cannot help but resent the process, as we feel the union of energy change again, and usually just when we thought we were coming up to a status quo on which we could relax slightly.

In order to let go of the feelings of impotence – frustration, sadness, fear of feeling disregarded – we will compare our standards with those of others to redress the balance. Occasionally, though, we will be shocked by what we find, as it can be such negatives as jealousy, selfish ambition or competitiveness, and so we will question our security and adequacy to cope. We may find it hard to relinquish control, and to refrain from trying to manipulate circumstances to what we consider to be the public good. It is always difficult to watch events unfold in a manner that we disagree with, when we believe that we could make things so much better with a little input and control, but nevertheless, that is what we must do. Not interfering allows us to relocate, redress and reunite all the disparate parts into a new form, more complete than ever before. It also provides time and space for every person to grow and glow in a manner that is effective within the total care system. That system is only understood partially and in hindsight, but the inner guidance works in foresight – so pay attention to it! The space we are permitting and being permitted at this time serves the purpose of allowing the two forces to meet in the here and now.

From this moment onwards, our meditation will yield results, and we must continue pushing ahead regardless of how difficult things are. Another era, another age, another meld of energies; we are in alignment and are in the process of clearing out old and irrelevant environmental residue, to be taught in a new way how to experience things. Life will go at quite a pace now, and we just need to remain calm, take each day as it comes, taking one step at a time. No more past, no more long distance future. Just now time!

Checklist:

- Do you have the desire to investigate the mystery that is within you and have you stated that desire aloud?
- Are you intending doing this work quietly?
- How do you intend to ask inside if you should study or consult with a person who will be made known to you, or do you intend a do-it-yourself effort?
- Who have you consulted and were they helpful, or did you do what you did on line?
- How would you consider you had made a start? Once you do, more will be added and things will start happening around you - take note.

12
LETTING GO IN TRUST AND ACCEPTANCE

When someone tyrannises, dictates, dominates or terrorises other people, they are using, abusing, hurting and harming fellow human beings. If a deeper level of history is recollected then suddenly we start to get into judgment, blame, criticism and condemnation, as a survival mechanism to protect ourselves against ill-treatment and revenge, which may or may not have been our experience in times gone by. Feelings of insecurity and/or inadequacy that we possess can cause us to impose a standard of self-protection from what we consider to be injustice; if we choose to liberate ourselves and love, even when we are not happy with the situation, we either avenge, when we appear to be aggressive and hostile, or we get suspicious and defensive, which makes us appear to be a soft touch. If we choose to attempt to raise the standards, then we surrender and let go of effluent harmlessly while retaining essence. If too quick a fix is attempted then we have to be careful not to waste resources, people or community assets. Otherwise it can easily lead to people being accident- prone or illness occurring as the toxins and waste can be too extreme to release and we are trying to move on too quickly. As an aside, this can cause bad lower leg pain and skin rashes.

If a more long-term investment is planned for the allocated space in nature's cycle, we may then try to fight or run away, but we find ourselves unable to do so; if we take one careful step after another we may feel the strain but we will prove capable of managing the growth required of us, as well as being able to harmonise with other people and all the kingdoms of nature. This will cause the pressure to be high enough to change anything, because opposites create the central pivot between fission and fusion, expansion and contraction. Within the void space, nature will organise and administer the orchestration of the new life and all will be ready to accommodate what is required.

People choose equality for all, but it must not be forgotten that each person will have their own skills and abilities, and time is required for everyone to find out where it is that they fit in the revised format, if they are included at all. However, remember that pushing too hard can reactivate persecution, and murder or suicide then become possibilities. If we are captivated by the past, it is easy to repeat it, as we know how to do that; much more difficult and pleasurable is to take responsibility for old behaviour, then convert it to something more loving and worthy of who we are now. It may not feel over-romantic but it is the real forward passage. If movement is too slow a revolution may inadvertently be incited, but it is important to be caring for all parties involved, even the slowest of all; never forget that speed of progress is individual and in a group situation we work at the rate the slowest is able to accommodate. We will hear, see and feel things that someone else cannot as yet – but it is also true that others will be more advanced than us, so have patience and compassion. If things are done the Management Upstairs' way, rather than the way of the subjective will, there will be enough light to see the way but not enough for it to be blinding. The darkness gains periods of rest, enough for mind and body to keep up with the soul purpose, and so the union becomes absolute. Within the sacred marriage is a possibility of a new direction, a new way of being with a new way of doing things. We need to recognise it is a celebration. Beyond a certain point in time there is just no room for sabotage or double agendas.

To hold a collective space in which many people play a part, opportunities will be given to all those people to import their own skill remit in collaboration with others. The soul journey of each will be played out along with the collective issue until there is a natural and easy conclusion that all understand. Some go on together, some join other groupings. Some have learned what they need to learn and they move one way, others need to repeat or relearn the collective lesson and will be seconded to other groups doing the same task. It is vital that all are safe enough to speak their truth; insecurities and vulnerabilities need to be aired without the persecution or sacrifice of any. It's crucial that honesty prevails along with integrity and an unselfishness that allows every person to take their turn in a loving, non-judgmental environment, and to feel safe and secure while doing so. Only then will movement be smooth and the new ways found. Free choice is offered as a result of which the Management Upstairs does what it can to maintain the purity of unconditional care of all.

Our new work is becoming a reality – one that will amaze and astound both us and countless others. There is no need to be surprised at the glorious lifestyle, though; it will make old pain fade into an insignificant backwater where others of like mind reside while we flow onwards. That process will allow the new to enter into our next work, which will involve the love and care of more multinational situations and incidents, be they within relationships, a residence or work. Having got this far into the book, you should know by now that past pain must be purged from the body and it does this through emotional and physical manifestations, which we have to endure. We may have old situations represented to us in an updated form to enable us to take another look and to decide if we wish to repeat or to release. Any pain and bruising on our left side at this period will be due to a few of the strategic moves from the past that brought upon us the wrath of others and from which we internalised the injustice. If the damage is on the right side it was more likely that our actions caused others pain, and forgiveness is required prior to our being free to move on again. These experiences are in the past now, so our body will need to find its own form of release. There will be no more using or abusing, bruising or battery, disrespect or dishonour, disloyalty or disregard, enslavement or service expectation, no infringement of universal law and no assumptions of greatness or self-importance. Repeat the following aloud:

I wish to treat others well and to be treated well. I wish to respect and be respected, to love and be loved.

Checklist:

- Do you feel able to live and let live?
- Do you feel the need to go to places where you know you are disliked or will be disrespected?
- Is it your intention to include all-comers as you welcome them into your space and to not visit those with whom there is no complementary feeling?
- Do you honour all those you work with to the best of your ability, treating them as equals?
- Do you feel ready and willing to serve and service what comes your way to the best of your ability?

13
LET THE MANAGEMENT MANAGE

As sentient beings, humans experience a number of negative emotions. When we hear the term 'negative emotion' we may immediately think of anger, frustration or being upset, but there are more: disillusionment, disappointment, feeling disregarded or dishonoured, betrayal, scepticism, cynicism, bitterness and sadness. All too often we seek others to blame, judge, criticise and condemn, misplacing our own feelings of inadequacy or feeling unimportant by projecting our pain onto someone else. Negativity need not be unwelcome for the deal is to create the cleansed and empty void in which a new and beautiful form is welcomed. We certainly know the sensation of feeling hurt, harmed or damaged but simultaneously wanting to avoid hurting, harming or damaging others. We cannot change the circumstances, but we can forgive and let go of resentment of others – and within this we must include ourselves. It is not possible to rescue or protect ourselves from the perceived pain of being. It may seem that we are first in and last out in most instances, and we cannot expect anyone else to understand – their experience of life is very different from our own. At a certain stage we will be gifted contact with teachers and colleagues - just enough for us to keep going.

This is something the Management Upstairs can, and will, help with, but we need to ask for the appropriate help. Help cannot be given unless or until we ask for it; it is a 'regulation' that the greater (more evolved) cannot override the will of the lesser (less evolved) until asked. Request that you and all others be freed and act as if, on this occasion, you require to be placed first in the queue. As we claim the "feel good" factor we celebrate, for our journey has been long and hard. No longer will we take on board the pain of others, the fear of others or the sadness that each has to find their way through. We might like to lighten their load but we can't.

Ask that the pain of all be replaced by forgiveness, interest, love and joy for everyone; and that old conflicts, grief, separations and divisions be let go of and all past behaviours that did not support, nurture, cherish or encourage everyone equally be gone once and for all. Ask that you be shown the way so that nobody feels used, abused, hurt or harmed and that you are at some point, somehow, also included. Read the following out loud as an affirmation:

I have no wish to be a living sacrifice to my peers and I have no wish to be punished by others. Please forgive me my inadequacies. If the Management Upstairs requires it, it will happen. I am fearful of disintegration, fearful of being mocked, scorned, ridiculed and condemned, but also fearful of being left out, uncared for, isolated or abandoned. So I fall and ask if what is disintegrated can be reintegrated; what is fragmented can be made whole once more.

When we have a strong desire to be a part of someone's life for good reasons, such as contributing to the lives of our children, then our love is unselfish, and when that other person, such as our child, desires that we act only in accordance with their codes of practice, it is a sign of their frustration on Earth and their apparent impotence. Do not fear, though – they will find their way in time, just as we found ours.

Our days of being hurt and harmed are now long gone; we have paid dearly for the hurt and harm that was inflicted on others by us, and now each must pay for the damage that they may have inflicted or experienced. We do not need to be involved.

Repeat the following:

May light light through me. May love love through me. May my body and mind exude goodwill. May my service be as is required. May my soul guide me. And thank you to Mother/Father/the Management Upstairs and Mother Nature.

Our next move is to learn to bless all people and events we come across, and that process is already in motion. Easy when warm, comfortable and of good cheer, not easy at all when we are unwell, cold or events appear to conspire to trip us up. What we believe we perceive, so we need to keep a check on our way of thinking, not only in our actions but in our reactions as well. So easy to gossip or comment on other people's affairs. We are never in full knowledge, nor do we know the path they are here to follow. Better we hold the boundaries of our space and we bless them in theirs as we extend our love.

We should now ask for permission and for guidance if we are to support and encourage others. More than that and the joint space can become unsustainable. Incorrect or dishonourable behaviour will attract the same towards us if we do not pay attention and take care. If we take charge and control people or events, more than just administering things effectively on behalf of the Management Upstairs, we will find ourselves in deep water. We can always request that Mother Nature help organise our space so no one is used, abused, dishonoured or dismissed until the Management Upstairs wants things to change. We must respect boundaries, our own and those of all others. We can change our attitude in relation to the time and effort that others give to us, and choose not to feel used, abused, victimised, prostituted, sacrificed, persecuted, jealous or competitive with regard to issues where the sacred balance appears not quite in partnership or balance. We also want to be careful that we do not use, abuse, hurt, harm, sacrifice, persecute or condone jealousy or competitive behaviour in ourselves or others.

There may have been, in our lives, specific people that we feel used or abused by, and others that have made us feel cherished, for such is the balance of things at times of profound learning. Do we feel that we lack the ability to assert ourselves as a result of having been undervalued in the past? If this is true, ask to be shown how to change your state so that you and others are treated fairly and never exploited by other people again. Ask for the level of love and respect you have earned to manifest itself within your life now, even as you continue to work to improve it.

As our understanding increases, our demarcation of boundaries must become more precise as our dedication to the service of the Management Upstairs while still on the earth begins to hold sway. People will seek us out and we must manage our time and our space to the best of our ability, being fair to ourselves, our family, our colleagues and clients. Our new work will soon take the place of the older way of operating. As the transition occurs we feel both stimulated and excited without really knowing why. We begin our round of farewells, and initially may feel disillusioned as we see some of our least desirable aspects and then wonder if we have made a strong enough contribution to other people. It is too late to go back, and too early to step forward; despite knowing this, we can suffer as a result if it is still bothering us. But it isn't a problem as we will be learning from the Management Upstairs, and all is now ready. We are now in transition and will shortly be receiving our new "orders". In the meantime, release all that is not essential and be at peace, knowing we are heading for a great future; we trust that this is so.

In the coming months there will be major happenings in the lives of everyone surrounding us, but rest assured that if those in our arenas have done their spiritual homework, they will not be unduly disrupted. As we see weather patterns, earth changes, political unrest, civil disturbance and so on begin to occur, it may include neighbours and colleagues from the past, and our task during this time will be to remain grounded and steady, while being involved and interested in everybody. They will be presented individually and be amazed at our ability to empathise with their points of view, which will then lead to unexpected involvement in unfamiliar areas, and this will both enthuse and stimulate them and us. We will find ourselves busy with events that make us happy and give comfort to others. We will never find ourselves pining for something to do.

The hostilities that are clinging on from the past must be laid to rest by people who are willing and able to see beyond the happenings of the present moment. The work of the next phase is to bring this awareness to those who are able to realise their own potential and also the potential that others have, and then declare a ceasefire. This is not always an easy task, though. Candid discussion is a luxury and frank negotiation is an impossibility, so all that is possible upon the Earth plane is social frivolity and light banter. The ability to hold and host spaces where the silence brings those from beyond our remit is now a skill which is sorely needed, as it allows us to mingle in areas that we have, up to now, been unable to master. From here, our next step will enter our consciousness with remarkable speed. The component parts are all in place and we will see how to proceed within the coming times with speed and ease. One more facet of our soul will present itself, enriching our whole living experience.

Our life on Earth no longer holds our previous identity; our updated one is an immense and luminous field that we are now linking into. It will permit us to reach many who are searching for another way of being. Our personality is one that is just the tool that attracts one to another; we express sincere interest in the ways of others, which boosts confidence for all concerned. As we stay still in the space, so all can be reached and 'held' as the spirit enters in more profoundly than ever before.

The Management Upstairs' work is being carried out and our next steps will find us busy, fulfilled and at peace. Our new form will include being available and willing to take instruction from the Management Upstairs as and when it is required.

We observe the way we have been manipulated and controlled by the desires of others but we are not worried about it anymore. We cooperate and comply because we are willing to see how everyone's input can make a difference – so do not think, or be bullied into thinking, that we are cooperating through fear or laziness, because nothing could be further from the truth. We will be richly rewarded for our positive attitude when we are able to make it our 'norm'.

The work of the Management Upstairs is carried out in subtle ways and all of our efforts will be greatly appreciated. We have passed the current test of initiation and achieved excellent marks, and now the world is, as they say, our oyster. We are free to proceed, as are all the other people involved. We can now obtain the necessary information and we will no doubt be stunned by how well we find out we have performed. No one has been harmed, and best of all, our future is safeguarded and will bear rich fruit. Our ability to report with accuracy and to negotiate at all levels of being is now assessed and all will benefit as a result, as we find placement for the next phase. We needed to be stretched and fatigued, as it could have meant we deviated from our path, but we did not – we remained strong. Be at peace, know that you are richly blessed, and keep on keeping on. Always.

CONCLUSION

Before reading on, congratulate yourself for getting this far. By taking the steps you have done to understand yourself and the world better, you have opened up a broader future of possibilities and happiness, not only for yourself, but also for those whom you encounter.

The real purpose of this book is to explain that the interior of us will be externalised, and inner and outer must unite and go in the same direction. God, the Greater, the Management Upstairs, or whatever your own personal name is for the powers that influence us from the invisible realities, needs to be lived and that is when we enjoy life the most, seeing all the amazing opportunities that are presented to us. Some people in life seem to 'have all the luck' – but there is nothing lucky about it at all, it is simply the positive result of having progressed and being an open, honest soul. Life cannot just pass us by, nor can we just hope to leave everything to the Management Upstairs – we must live life, and we must play a very active role in our destiny. The key factor, though, is being united with the Management Upstairs in a common intention. That is what will make a huge difference to us.

One of the central messages of this book is about change – shedding the old, learning new things and embracing those changes. Change is vital and occurs throughout life – puberty is a change, leaving school and getting a job is a change, and so on – but that does not mean it is easy. Just as we know we must learn but loathe the learning experience itself, change can be difficult but it is fundamental to growth and a happy existence. It is hard, but so worthwhile! If we live giving service to others then our lives will change dramatically, but only in a positive way. There is nothing to lose and everything to gain! Remember that for there to be light at the end of the tunnel, we must be able to work in the dark. It can be a good metaphor for life, in fact – we start in the womb and travel down the dark birth canal into the light of life. It is necessary to travel through the dark to enter the light, and that is a key message that we should always remember, especially at moments of difficulty in life.

We all know how difficult life can be, but hindsight often makes us see the bigger picture and that it wasn't so bad after all. If we could make hindsight foresight then we could have fewer qualms about doing certain things. So, to that end, here is a brief breakdown of the stages that we will all find ourselves going through and what to expect:

- We take up a discipline, such as a martial art or yoga.

- We may have a mystical or psychic experience – is it real or imagined?

- "What shall I do with it?" we ask. Options include signing into a psychiatric hospital, consulting a medic, joining a religious community, etc. At this moment the spiritual gift feels like a curse.

- There is a loss, perhaps of community, and a feeling of being judged or criticised. "Is it us or them?" we wonder. We feel odd.

- We handle our own rebellion and try to be disciplined, as well as obedient to instruction. We love and hate it at the same time.

- We decide what to do with what the Management Upstairs gives us, and we try to create a structure.

- We learn the new codes and ethics, deciding if our conscience will be able to cater to the old and new, the past and future, the mystical and the Earth.

- We learn how to fix things, bring the mystical down and the life standards up, while simultaneously filtering the past and honouring existing dynamics. We must be flexible and give permission for change.

- We free all others so that we all may pursue our own course.

- We avoid being resentful or bitter despite life being so relentless – we feel like a stone in the centre of a field during lashing rain and high winds.

- Uncertainty. The spiritual gamble and the life gamble. "Will I be accepted and acceptable, or will I be rejected by others?" We need the courage to walk into the unknown and do what we feel we have to do. We start to regain our sense of humour and laugh more while crying much less.

- We feel gentleness and peace, rest and recovery. New challenges are welcomed.

- Help and support arrive in some form and lets us make sense out of apparent nonsense.

Such is the breakdown, and when viewed like that it is not so intimidating, as it converts into a major breakthrough. Once we know where we are and what comes next – and, more importantly, how good the outcome will be – we have renewed vigour and can knuckle down.

Heed the guidance and lessons in the book to unlock your own full potential. There will be moments of sadness, anger and discouragement, but remember that each step takes you closer to the goal, and you will experience joy, happiness and purpose that far exceed anything you have ever felt in your life before.

Embrace everything, and make the most of each opportunity that comes your way.

Lightning Source UK Ltd.
Milton Keynes UK
UKOW03f0259181113

221263UK00006BB/129/P